# PREFACE

AS I WRITE this book, I'm 78-years-old and Vietnam was more than half a century ago. I still have dreams about being in Vietnam – not really nightmares, just normal dreams – although things change in the dreams, the same way they do in other dreams. Talking about my time in Vietnam has never been a problem for me. That year helped me grow up. It gave me some discipline. It was a time in my life that helped make me who I am. I would never want to forget about that. Sure, there were bad things that I lived through, but in many ways, Vietnam wasn't as bad as high school. Both were about surviving and growing up. At least in Vietnam I knew who the enemy was and what they wanted.

Despite my willingness to talk about that experience, I had never considered it in the context of a book. So, why did I decide to compile this memoir? Well, good friends of mine, Ty and Karen Pierce, suggested that a memoir would be worthwhile after learning that I still had all the letters I wrote home from Vietnam to my then new bride and to my parents. Ty is a man I mentored as his coach and he is as close to me as a son and I value and respect his opinion.

We were talking about time in the army and I brought out the box of letters for them to flip through. My wife and my parents had kept all the letters I wrote to them while I was in the military from 1966 to 1968, from basic training through my return from Vietnam. I didn't expect them to read as many as they did. When they found them to be interesting, even enthralling, they suggested the idea of a book. I resisted at first, figuring that no one else would find them to be as interesting as Ty and Karen did. But they were pretty emphatic about the idea. When my wife Beth encouraged me, too, I started to come around and warm up to the notion. The four of us went through all the letters and got them ready for use in the writing of the book.

This is a history, not written fifty-five years later, but written when it happened in the form of letters. Day by day, week by week, month by month, through the eyes of an infantryman.

Many of the names of my fellow soldiers are no longer familiar to me and their faces are long forgotten. At the time, I probably only knew about half of the men in the company. Even so, there are a few that I remember well, some of them even fondly. I haven't had much contact with any of them over the decades, although I know what became of a small number of them.

Rereading the letters and writing this book did bring back many memories, images, sounds, smells, and tastes. It also brought back emotions, the strongest being how much I missed Beth and looked forward to being home with her again for good.

She contributed to some of the chapters, the ones she had first-hand involvement in, as she has contributed to everything in my life. If it wasn't for her, most of my life wouldn't have been what it was. If I didn't have her waiting for me, my tour in Vietnam might have gone very differently. In any case, I wouldn't have had many of the letters that became this book, if she hadn't been in my life. Sure, I also wrote to my parents, but there were many things I told Beth that I didn't tell them.

When I returned home, I put the war behind me. I have been an artist, coach, and fisherman. I coached junior high boys football and basketball and high school girls basketball. Hopefully, I had a positive impact on the lives of many young people over the years. As an artist, I paint southwestern themes and nature that have often been described as beautiful and inspiring. I competed in bass fishing for nine years after retiring.

My hope is that, like coaching and painting, this book will leave people with a positive response. My former players who may read this book will see a side of me that they never knew about. How that will affect their view of me, I don't know. Some might be surprised by these stories. Others may not. I can only present the information and let people react however they will.

# LETTERS
## *from*
# *Vietnam*

DENNIS HOY

Also, I am part Potawatomi Indian, "the people of the place of the fire," and am proud of that heritage. The Potawatomi teach their children about the Seven Grandfather Teachings of wisdom, respect, love, honesty, humility, bravery, and truth. I hope that my story reflects pieces of each of these teachings and might inspire fellow Native Americans. I hope it may further help bring some recognition of that fact that we have served in the military at a higher per capita rate than any other ethnic group. Approximately 42,000 Native Americans served during the Vietnam War. Of these, 90% were volunteers, while I was part of the 10% who were drafted. I am grateful to the Potawatomi Nation for honoring me at its Citizen Cultural Heritage Center in Shawnee, Oklahoma, where its Wall of Honor has a section dedicated to the 250 Citizen Potawatomi who were Vietnam veterans, the largest enlistment of the Potawatomi tribe in any American foreign conflict.

Maybe other veterans will be comforted by my stories, or at least find humor in them, because there was a lot of humor in the army and in the war, which many people may find surprising. Veterans from all eras may be able to relate to what I endured and sometimes enjoyed. For those without a military background, my stories may give you valuable insights into a soldier's mentality, experience, and perspective – at least this soldier's.

# CHAPTER 1

ON FEBRUARY 27, 1967, I landed in Bien Hoa, Vietnam, on the edge of Saigon. Immediately, the heat and humidity hit me. Although it was still technically winter, the temperature was in the high 90s, maybe over 100 degrees. It felt worse than that, though, because of the humidity. Little did I know that February was one of the least humid months of the year.

From the airport, we were bused a few miles to Long Binh, the largest U.S. Army base in Vietnam, with tens of thousands of troops. There was no welcoming committee of any sort and no one really seemed to care where I went or what I did as I awaited orders assigning me to my unit in the field. I just had to go to a certain building periodically to check the list of assignments. That was the full formality of the process – look at a list of names posted on a bulletin board, wondering when mine would magically appear. Beside the names were the field assignments. Until my name was on the list, I had nothing to do. I wasn't in a big hurry to go anywhere anyway. No one was shooting at me in Long Binh, so I didn't mind if they took their sweet time assigning me to a unit.

It was nice to at least have a chance to shower and get a shave in the barbershop. The barber was a local, so you could say I had my first close shave with a Vietnamese. Honestly, it was a little scary having him hold a razor to my neck, but it went fine.

Long Binh is a suburb of Saigon, on the northeast edge of the city, a 22-mile drive from the city center. It's about 30 miles from the South China Sea, which contributed to the humidity. After the shower, I was quickly covered in sweat again. Even the night temperatures only got down to the high 70s. Those of us who were waiting assignments stayed in a big tent with the sides drawn up to let air in, maybe cooling it down a little. On top of the temperature and humidity, it also rained quite a bit.

While I was here, I recorded a taped message to Beth. I had brought a tape recorder with me for this purpose. We had the notion of sending tapes back and forth, sort of having a conversation. That didn't work out as we had hoped once I got to the field. In this first message, I told her that I had started growing a mustache, then ran out of tape before I could say goodbye. I wasn't accustomed yet to watching when the tape would run out. One could hear firing and mortar rounds going off, bombs and artillery fire in the distance, jets landing and taking off every few minutes. All that noise probably wasn't very comforting for Beth to hear, but there was no way for me to keep it off the recording.

I said earlier that I had nothing to do at Long Binh. Officially, that wasn't true. In theory, every night I was supposed to be on KP (kitchen patrol – usually that meant washing dishes). In reality, I only showed up once briefly, so they knew I was there. I left and never went back. As far as I know, nobody missed me. The reason I could get away with this was the sheer number of men here. We were all able to just not show up for details. After all, we were only there for a couple of days and they'd have to come find us among the thousands of people. It just wasn't possible or even worth it to them. What are they going to do? Send me to Nam?

This flood of soldiers was a direct result of General Westmoreland, commander of Military Assistance Command, Vietnam (MACV), asking Congress for a hundred thousand men. I was part of the hundred thousand requested. We were rushed through basic training and then Advanced Individual Training (AIT) and were shipped to Vietnam, with thousands of people showing up all the time.

After two days, my name finally appeared on the list and I learned that I had been assigned to the 1st Cavalry Division. This would not have been my first choice. They were frequently mentioned in the news as being in firefights. Until that moment, I had held on to hope that my assignment would be somewhere relatively safe – not that anywhere in Vietnam was safe, which was proven by all the harassment fire every night at Long Binh. I guess I knew, though, that infantrymen didn't get the safe assignments. The safe assignments went to what we referred to as "clerks and jerks." Grunts like me got the 1st Cav. Specifically, I was assigned A Company, 1st Battalion, 5th Cavalry Regiment, 1st Cavalry Division (Airmobile).

The 1st Cav had a history in the Korean War and my understanding was that they didn't have a good reputation for what they had done there. I didn't really know what had happened, but what I had heard wasn't very flattering. Their unit shoulder patch was yellow with a black diagonal slash across it and a horse in the corner. And what people said was that yellow is the color of your back, the slash was the river you never crossed, and the horse was the one you never rode. So, that was their reputation. What the army does with a lot of the units with a reputation like that is put them in conditions where they have to prove themselves again, to build their reputation back up – at least that was the scuttlebutt among soldiers. That's what I now found myself in the middle of at the start of my combat tour. The 1st Cav was the first full American division committed to Vietnam and had arrived in September 1965, so they'd been in country about a year and a half by the time I joined them.

They were called "airmobile," which referred to their helicopter assets. Moving troops around by helicopter was a new style of combat in Vietnam that every division used – 1st Cav, the Big Red 1, and all of the others. It was faster and more responsive than having to travel long distances by truck or by foot. The difference is that most divisions had to request helicopter support from external aviation units. In contrast, 1st Cav had its own internal helicopters. This made them immediately available to our troops. So, if we needed a helicopter, we just got on the radio and called them and they were there. This capability transformed the 1st Cav into kind of the elite force in Vietnam, because of their enhanced capabilities. It gave them more mobility than other divisions, shorter reaction times, and even more firepower, thanks to the weapons onboard the helicopters.

Now that I had my assignment, things happened quickly. I was put on a transport plane, along with the other new 1st Cav soldiers, and flown over 300 miles to the northeast, to the town of An Khe, where the division headquarters was. This was in the central highlands of Vietnam about a third of the way up the country from south to north or about halfway between Saigon and the "border" with North Vietnam.

Upon arriving in An Khe, we spent another day waiting to be distributed to different battalions. Because this was the division base camp, the facilities were a little more built up than where I would soon find myself. Here, we had barracks to sleep in with bunk beds and even mosquito netting. It was very posh by field standards. We were issued our jungle fatigue uniforms, jungle boots, rifle, plus all the other "junk" that goes with it. In other words, all the added weight I would have to carry around with me. It's a very mountainous country, generally with thick jungle vegetation, and this gear was better suited to that terrain.

So, I was issued my jungle stuff: helmet, ammo, "web gear," and everything else – too many items to list or even remember. I liked An Khe. It was really nice. It was completely different than basic and AIT, in that we didn't have to stand at attention and be constantly harassed or anything. We were just there to get a job done. Then, they let you sleep until 7:00 and sit around whenever you want, not like at Fort Polk where I did my training. (Things were about to change.) There was good food and lots of it. We received extra pay – per diem, travel pay, combat pay. I had $90 in my pocket, so I went to the PX to buy a watch. I got a Bulova for $55 that retailed for $68. So far, war was working out pretty well for me.

On March 3, I learned that I would have to go to a special school for three days. After basic and AIT, what more training did the army think I needed?

We were told that the company would be coming to An Khe the next day. When they arrived, a brass band played and there was a big celebration. I was assigned to 1st Platoon. Artillery shells were fired, which they were always doing at An Khe. We had steak and beer, a big party, it was a really good time. The officers and enlisted men drank and ate together. A lot of soldiers drank too much and passed out and were carried off to the barracks, not me though. The captain thought it was funny. I sat by myself and ate a steak and drank a few beers. I got to meet a few of the men and they seemed nice.

A couple days later, we started hearing rumor that the company would be moving out soon, going back into the field. We'd be going to a place that I called, in my letters to Beth, Antelope Valley. The actual name is An Lao Valley and it was a large area about 20-30 miles north of An Khe. Before I moved out, though, I would be attending the school I was told about a few days ago. In this school, which is conducted on the base, those of us who were new to the company would receive specialized training to prepare us for the field in Vietnam.

On the first day of the three-day school, we practiced rappelling from a helicopter from 26-feet above the ground. Rappelling is a way of inserting soldiers into an area that presents no spot for a helicopter to land, either due to vegetation or terrain. So, the helicopter hovers while the soldiers slide down ropes hanging from both sides of the aircraft. One man is on the rope at a time, attached to it by carabiners, or what we called snaplinks, which the rope loops through. The friction of the rope through the snaplinks, along with the man's hands on the rope and the drag of the rope across his hip, helps control the speed of descent. Offsetting all of that, the weight of our gear adds to the speed. Sometimes, we might land with a thud – or worse. Better to make those mistakes in training than on a mission. Because rappelling has to be done one person at a time from each side, it's much slower than landing and everyone hopping out at once.

On the second day of class, we practice patrolling techniques, including learning the distinct standard operating procedures (SOPs) of the unit. For today, the training is conducted within the perimeter of the base. Tomorrow, the patrol training would take place outside the perimeter and we would spend the night out on patrol and come back in the next day, the fourth and final day of the school.

It's less than two weeks since arriving in Vietnam and I'm already getting low on stationery. I ask Beth to send me more.

Our company moved out while we were on our second day of school, so we would join them after completing training, on Sunday, March 12. They were in Bong Son, part of the An Lao region, but toward the ocean. It was a mountainous area with lots of heat and humidity. There was also a lot of enemy activity. My life was about to get more difficult. If war is hell, I was about to enter hell.

# CHAPTER 2

I ARRIVED AT MY platoon at about 3:30 in the afternoon, flown in along with hot chow. That was one good thing about the Air Cav having organic aircraft, they would often fly in hot chow to the troops in the field as they were settling in for the night. They didn't do this every night, but often. Otherwise, it's cold C rations, which is what we get for breakfast and lunch. I was told that I could have some hot chow only if there was some left after everyone else had eaten. Fortunately, they didn't eat it all and I got to eat.

My squad was going on ambush that night. My squad leader asked the captain what to do with me, since I was so new. He said, "Well, take him and break him in." So, they broke me in.

We went down the mountain and back up it, quite a long hike. I was tense, naturally. The other guys appeared to be more accustomed to being in this sort of danger, but this was new to me and the conditions made it even worse. It was getting pretty dark. There was no moon and the sky was overcast, so we didn't even have starlight. Because of this, it was even more difficult than usual to spot any other signs of danger. I was trained to always be looking around for the enemy, but in this darkness, I wouldn't have seen them if they were much more than an arm's length away from me. I also couldn't see the other men in the squad from the normal distance of ten yards, so we had to follow each other at a shorter distance. In training, we're told to keep ten yards apart so that a grenade blast would only hit one of us. I was about to learn how true that was.

When we were almost at our objective, our point man hit a booby trap – a trip wire attached to some sort of explosive device. I was the fourth man back and the blast shook me, even ten to twenty yards back. The point man and the next man back were both hurt, so we called for a medevac, which is a medical helicopter which we call for by radio to evacuate injured soldiers and take them to the nearest medical facility for treatment. Other soldiers in the squad administered basic first aid to the two injured men, as we were all trained to do. The rest of us faced outward in a circle, in case the enemy attacked. The medevac arrived and we helped load the two casualties quickly onto the helicopter, which took off again within what seemed like only a minute.

We settled in for the night at that spot, continuing to be on watch for any threats, but nothing happened. The next morning, on the way back from ambush, we ran into two more booby traps. Fortunately, in the daylight, they were both detected before they were tripped. We blew both of them up, so they wouldn't cause someone else any harm.

We were by the South China Sea in the vicinity of Bong Son. Sitting on top of a mountain, looking directly out at the sea just a few miles away, I looked down in the valleys where they grew rice and had rivers running through them. There was fog rolling in from the sea, so it would probably be damp tonight. The mountains were very pretty and the jungles were thick and lush. It's hard to believe that such an awful war was going on in such a beautiful place.

We were waiting for the helicopters to come in and pick us up. We were going to make an air attack on a company of VC (Viet Cong) that hit the 2nd and 5th Cav Battalions yesterday and did quite a bit of damage to them. We were going to try and hit them back.

All this information about where we're going or what we're doing is passed down from the company down to the platoons. What I'm describing is what was related to me from the people in that platoon. It's like playing a game of telephone. By the time the information reaches me, the original truth might be completely lost – or maybe not. I can't say for sure that all this was accurate, but it's as accurate as I know it to be.

It was not lost on me that on my very first patrol of the war, my first day on a combat mission, we had two men injured enough to require medevac. At least they weren't killed. It was a very big first day and night in the field and I had the thought that this was going to be a long year. I'm 24 years old and one of the oldest soldiers in our company, excluding the captain, sergeant majors, and a few other lifers. Statistics showed that most deaths and injuries occurred to the soldiers in the first month or in the last month in Vietnam. The first month, because they don't know what is going on and, a lot of times, they don't know what to do. The last month, because they are "short" – near the end of their one-year tour – and become too cautious or too careless.

When I first went over there, they started rotating you to the rear to go home 30 days before it was time for you to go. Then, we got a new captain and he cut it down to 15 days. The last captain I had cut it down to seven days before you could go back.

My service number starts "US," which means that was drafted. "RA" (Regular Army) means you joined or volunteered. "NG" means they are National Guard. None of which are over here, in Vietnam. They were in basic training and then went home to serve in their Guard unit. I believe they had to be in the National Guard for six to eight years. I'm not sure about that. If you were drafted, you have to serve two years. Regular Army joined for maybe four years.

On the next day, Monday, March 13, our platoon is being used as a blocking force, so we don't have to move, just sit tight and let the other three platoons drive the enemy toward us. The company is made up for four platoons – four firing squads per platoon – plus the command group. One of the platoons is a mortar platoon, the other three are rifle platoons. The command posts and mortar platoons always stay together. The rifle platoons can go on missions by themselves. Most of the times we move from one spot to the next spot as a company, but sometimes when you're moving from one spot to another spot, the rifle platoons would each take three different paths and we'd all meet up together. We never stayed in the same place more than a day. We were in search and destroy, trying to find the enemy and then we'd have a place we'd set up and we'd camp in for that night. We'd either secure the perimeter, be on listening posts. or go on ambush. You'd do one of the three and rotate each night. So, you never stayed in the same place long at all.

Most of the time, we'd get up in the morning and have orders and the captain would bring us together and tell us, this is what we're doing. Usually, we moved from one place to another place as a company by itself.

Last night, we witnessed an air strike and an artillery bombardment on the mountain across from us 500 to 300 meters away – quite a show. One artillery round hit about 50 meters from my foxhole. My lieutenant got on the radio and chewed them out. You had to make sure the gunners understand that their aim is off before the next round is fired, or it might be too late. This morning started out with another air raid and artillery shelling. There's artillery and mortar shelling every night.

One of the ammo bearers had to go back to base camp last night to do something – he was also a new guy – and now I had to carry his ammo for the machine gun, as well as the one I was already carrying, which made two. When you were new, you had to carry all the ammo for the machine guns and you got all the other dirty details (jobs). You were low man on the totem pole. My own gear – backpack and all – weighed around 80 pounds. Each can of ammo weighed around 20 pounds. Needless to say, I was not happy to have to carry the extra weight. I looked forward to the arrival of the next new recruit.

I was dirty and hadn't been able to bathe in a stream (there were no showers out there). I took my boots off for the first time in six days. Everybody had a poncho to keep the rain off of him. We took our ponchos, snapped two of them together, and had a bamboo pole and stakes in the ground, it made our tents. And, we had air mattresses to sleep on, if they didn't have holes poked in them from the stickers, and we had little blankets. We slept with our clothes on because, if a firefight broke out, we don't have time to put our boots on or dress or anything, so we were already dressed. There were three of us to a foxhole, one on guard for two hours, then four hours of sleep – the three of us rotated.

Even the plants could be our enemy. There were thorns out there we called "wait a minute." When we got stuck on one, we'd say, "wait a minute," because that's how long it'd take us to get unhooked by it.

Elephant grass could grow as high as 12 feet and was sharp. Hacking our way through that was a lot of work and could be painful.

We gave our letters to the door gunner when they'd fly out hot chow and he would mail it for us. We also let them know what resupply we needed, more ammo usually. Whatever things we needed, we'd tell the platoon sergeant and he sent it up to the command post and they'd send new stuff the next night or whenever the next helicopter came out. It wasn't a perfect system, but it worked pretty well.

Okay, I need to talk about what I carried with me. I keep thinking people know what I carried, but really, people are usually shocked to learn how much soldiers carry during combat.

I had a backpack fastened on an aluminum frame. I had a poncho that was used to keep the rain off of us. I also had a blanket made out of something synthetic, which makes it real light. C rations and extra ammo went in the backpack. Also, we had a plastic helmet liner and over that went the steel pot, the outer metal part of the helmet. Another important – but heavy – item was the entrenching tool, or foldable shovel. We had web gear, which was a web belt with suspenders. On the web gear, two canteens of water were attached – I later carried five – ammo pouches, 15 magazines that held 20 rounds each. We were told to put only 18 rounds in them, so the spring inside didn't get too compressed to activate the next bullet up. That's 300 rounds for the M16. We carried an initial 200 rounds in small cardboard boxes that the ammo came in. That's a total of 500 rounds. I would later carry 700 rounds, most were tracer rounds. Three hand grenades, one smoke grenade, first aid bandage, and all of this fit on the web gear in ammo pouches or other types of cases. Several times, I really enjoyed that we could leave our pack where we'd dug in for the night and just wear our web gear with all that stuff on it. In the morning, sometimes, the helicopter would come in and we'd put all of our packs in the cargo net and they'd fly it to us that night, wherever we set up, so we didn't have to carry that damn pack all the time. Those days were like a dream come true.

Our helmet had a camouflage cover on it, held by an elastic strap. (This is kind of funny, but important.) That strap also held a plastic bottle of mosquito repellent. You had to have it on your helmet where it can be seen by the officers. It was supposed to keep the mosquitoes off of you. If you did not have it, you could be given an Article 15 (disciplinary action and fine). You had to use it, because that's how you got malaria, from the mosquitos. It was the little things like this that the army obsessed about. We were worried about getting shot and they worried about us getting bit by a mosquito.

We did not have extra socks or underwear or change of clothes. You wore what you had. I learned that you did not wear socks or underwear. They would get wet and were the last thing to dry out. We would use the socks to put C rations in and then tie them on the back of our packs or on our web gear. C rations came in little cardboard boxes. You can take them out of the boxes and put them in your socks on your pack and then you had more room inside your pack. If you needed new socks, you had to turn in an old pair – in pairs, not single socks. If I needed any new clothing – socks, pants, shirt – I had to turn in the old one to get a new one. I could order a new one, but I couldn't get it without turning in the old one.

We were also given heat tablets to heat up the C rations. You would take an empty C ration can, usually one that a roll or dessert came in because they were smaller, and using a beer opener, poke holes around the bottom of the can and put your heat tablet in it and light it. Open your new C ration can and leave the lid on to use as a handle and put it on your makeshift stove. That's how you heated up your food. We had a "P24" can openers that came with the C rations to open the C ration cans. I carried mine on my dog tag chain, a neat little instrument. I still have it on my dog tags. I'm sure there was more stuff I carried in my pack, but that about does it. No change of clothes.

On March 15th, my fire squad was sent out to set up an observation post on a mountain top. We had to cross two mountains to get to our destination. It was so hot that one guy passed out and two could hardly walk. It was brutal. On top of the heat, my legs were aching from the up and down trekking. That 80 pounds felt like a ton. I didn't want to think about what would have happened if we had run into VC near the end of that hike. Luckily, we didn't.

The VC were out there, though. From our higher vantage point, we watched another company sweeping the valley below us and the Vietcong running away ahead of them. We radioed that company and passed along the enemy routes. We called them VC, Vietcong, or Charlie. From our perspective, they are the North Vietnamese army. They have uniforms, helmets, and good weapons. And I still called them VC, even those who were officially part of the regular army from North Vietnam, NVA.

On March 18, I made my second air assault. Air assault just means we were transported to a battle area by helicopter. Airlift and airmobile mean the same thing. This was a means of insertion that became common in the Vietnam war for the first time. The way these operations were executed is that we'd go in two helicopters at a time, usually eight total for the fire squads – a bunch of helicopters go in, counting everyone. The first two are gunships. They are each armed with two rocket launchers, 48 rockets total, and two M60 machine guns. This is what I'm told that they had, and this may be an early version. They came out later with another version, a really sophisticated helicopter. Ours were just regular helicopters with rocket pods mounted on them. They'd go in firing rockets and machine guns at all enemy targets that they could identify, really soften up the area for us and maybe weaken the morale and resolve of the Vietcong.

Then, the first wave of soldiers would come in and secure the area for the rest of the ships that come in, the rest of the company. On my first air assault, I was on the second wave, so the area was already secured. On this one, I was in the first wave, so our squad had to secure the area, which meant searching for enemy, so we'd know if it was safe for the next wave to land. When the chopper gets about five feet from the ground, we started jumping off. The jungle was so thick that we had to chop our way through it. As we did that, we came upon a recently vacated VC stronghold with dug-in bunkers.

The sergeant told another guy who had been in Vietnam for some time to take me and search the area. The two of us searched the bunkers, weapons pointed wherever we looked, with our eyes lined up down the sights, ready to pull the trigger in a split second. The VC appeared to have just left the area, probably minutes earlier as they heard our helicopters approaching. It was real spooky knowing that we had just missed them. When we crossed a stream, we could see that the water was still filling their footprints. You almost can't miss them by less than that. I could actually still smell them. They smelled like charcoal, because they cooked a lot with charcoal. I'm sure they recognized our smell, too. Humans have distinct odors.

The Vietcong won't fight unless they have the advantage or are cornered. So, most of the time, we chased them to get them in a position where they would fight. It didn't make any difference how big or small a force they were. Make them fight, draw them into an engagement. We have enough support to come in with air power and artillery and we can usually do pretty good. That's why our tactics were more aggressive, search and destroy rather than hit and run. We had confidence in our superior firepower. We might not win every skirmish and we didn't always finish unscathed, but overall, we knew the bigger engagements would go our way.

We got down to a valley where there was a cold stream running and I took a good, cold bath. While we were vulnerable there, a VC threw a grenade down on us. Fortunately, it landed short. He should have never done that. We took care of the problem and didn't even need artillery this time. In this instance, M16s were superior firepower enough. Once that was settled, helicopters came in and took us back to the top of the mountain.

It may seem odd that I would bathe immediately after assaulting an enemy position, but when we found a stream and there was no clear threat, we had to take advantage of the rare opportunity. The way we did it in our platoon was like this. One soldier carried the bar of soap and one carried a razor and we shared everything. Half the squad would stand guard while the other half bathes. Then, we'd switch. You'd start with your shirt and wash it while you wore it, then your pants. After washing them, you'd take them off, rinse them off, and throw them on rocks. Hopefully, there are rocks. Then, you wash yourself, rinse off, and put your wet clothes back on. They will dry off while you walk, plus it cools you off. All of this took just a few minutes. It was our only option besides not bathing, which wasn't an option if you wanted to stay healthy, somewhat comfortable, and tolerably smelly.

I wrote two letters to Beth dated March 20. In one, I wrote about naming the new puppy she got Baron. There were also some comments about coming in second in archery.

In the other letter, I described checking out a huge VC complex of caves and tunnels. The Vietcong often operated out of underground complexes, which made it hard to find them and even harder to fight them. Thankfully, we didn't have to fight them this time. We did find the rice they left and papers with VC names that were probably helpful to the military intelligence people.

The squad leader had offered me the RTO position (radio-telephone operator). RTO was a position of responsibility, because being able to effectively communicate with the company command, call of air support, or request a medevac would be a matter of life and death for my squad mates (and me). Another consideration is that the VC knew all this and, therefore, would sometimes target the RTO. I said I would think about it.

The letter had a few other tidbits. While waiting to be air lifted to LZ English we played a game of football. We won 42 to 14 and I threw seven touchdowns. I had my first coconut and it was good. I found two ticks on me and burned them off. The small events were part of life in war and were just as important as the battles, sometimes. They provided color to an otherwise drab life.

In a letter March 24, I wrote to Beth about chasing Charlie and hitting him pretty bad. We had him boxed in. I thought we were in An Lao Valley, but we were in Bong Son province. We had been walking in rice paddies and crossing rivers waist deep for the past two days.

That same day, I wrote a letter to Bud, my Dad, to clear up what I had written previously. It was about our big battle that we fought on March 20. I wrote two letters to Beth on the 20th, which must have been before we were air lifted into that battle. I had written a first letter to Bud telling him about the battle. I told him if he felt that Beth could handle it, then show her the letter. Later, Beth wrote to me saying that Bud almost had a nervous breakdown from reading what I had told him about the battle. And from then on, I should write to her and if she thought Bud could handle it, she would tell him. I guess I was mistaken about who could handle what. I would not make that mistake again and Beth would prove throughout my time in Vietnam and the rest of our life together that she could handle more than most people can.

# CHAPTER 3

BEFORE I GET into the story of the big battle, I want to describe want led up to Vietnam and the training that was supposed to prepare me for battles such as this one.

I arrived at basic training, my introduction to the army, at the beginning of September. It was a two-month course at Fort Bliss, which is headquartered in El Paso, Texas, and extends into New Mexico. It's a huge base that spreads over 2,000 square miles, larger than the state of Delaware. It's the second largest army base after White Sands Missile Range. I would only know a small piece of that base. Basic training, or boot camp, was followed by Advanced Individual Training, or AIT, at Fort Polk in western Louisiana, a much smaller base, for three months into late January.

I'll start by mentioning Sargent Denbowski, a short (5'6") German, non-commissioned officer (NCO) who had to approve my first leave. I had brought Beth down to Fort Bliss for the weekend and just wanted to hurry up and get off base, so I could spend as much time as possible with her. This son of a bitch kept me in his office for several hours, waiting for his authorization. I finally paid him $20 for my pass. I will never forget his name. He's a sorry individual for treating a subordinate that way, for no reason other than to feel what limited power he had. All the sergeants harassed us as part of the training, but this guy was just an ass for no reason. The worst part was the thought of keeping Beth waiting for all those hours without being able to even tell her what was going on.

The purpose of basic training, as far as I could tell, was to relieve us of all individualism and make us react to all commands without a question. (Good luck.) We marched to commands. Did PT to commands. Even woke up and went to bed to commands. We did 10-mile marches, day and night, had inspection of our individual lockers, qualified with weapons, pulled KP (everyone got at least one duty of KP), and did meaningless duties like policing the area (picking up trash). They'd line us all up and have us walk across an area picking up anything that didn't belong or didn't grow. The drill sergeant would walk behind us, checking if we missed anything. If he found any little thing, he'd make us start again, but this time in a duck walk position. We'd go through it again. If he found anything we missed, we'd go back and line up and go again, this time in a low crawl (belly to the ground, using arms and legs to move forward). This would get us closer to the ground, so we wouldn't miss anything. This is the kind of stuff that we had to go through all the time in basic training. They supposedly broke us down to build us up again as soldiers. That was the theory anyway.

I made very few friends in basic training. One was Jessie Firestone from Melrose, New Mexico, a town of a few hundred people about 20 miles west of Clovis, where Beth and I lived. He was smarter than most of us and he was continuously screwing off. At the end of basic, he was sent to Fort Huachuca, Arizona, to be a truck driver. The rest of us ended up being in the Infantry, which is why I said he was smarter than us. When we were policing an area, he would stick his head in a bush. A lieutenant or sergeant would ask him what he's doing and he'd answer that he was looking for bugs. He was always doing stuff like, just to amuse himself. That was the kind of guy he was.

A little later history about him. When he returned to civilian life after the army, he went to work on the railroad, where he had a railroad car run over his finger and cut it off. The railroad paid him X amount of dollars for the "accident." I don't think it was an accident, from my understanding, but a way to get some free money. Personally, I'd rather have all of my fingers and not go through the pain of getting one run over by a railroad car. He then became a crop duster. I painted a picture of his plane for him. Later in life. I learned from the national news that he and his wife settled down in Arizona and had what was described as a compound. It seems to have been in trouble with drugs for some time. They had a confrontation with the police or Sheriff's office. He boobytrapped his compound with dynamite. And when the authorities arrived, he blew himself and his wife up. Jesse was 65 and his wife, Diedre, was 45. It was a senseless death and I don't understand what led up to it. I was sorry to hear that his life ended in this way.

Basic was a mix of actual military skills training and pointless activities. We started with having our heads shaved, getting issued our uniforms and gear, followed by a full day of KP duty, maybe just to set the tone from Day 1. The next day we had a 10-mile march. We did a lot of exercise – which a few of the guys really needed – and repeated inspections of our barracks and equipment. We had a good amount of weapons training on live fire ranges. We all had to get qualified on the M16, the basic rifle of the army infantryman at the time. Learning to shoot accurately was probably the most valuable training we received, the most relevant to fighting and surviving in Vietnam. I was pretty good at it and picked it up quickly. I had done a lot of archery, which has some of the same principles, so that helped. Obviously, there are some differences, but I adapted easily.

Let me say a little bit about PT, physical training, the way the army did it. Later in life, after I got back from service, I became a physical education teacher and I used some of these commands and did the same things. It's almost like Simon Says. For example, exercise number one would be Jumping Jacks and the starting position of Jumping Jacks is the position of attention. And so, it would go something like this. "Exercise number one, Jumping Jacks. Starting position, move!" I would put my arms above my head, being the leader, and if any of the students put their arms above their heads, they would have to do ten pushups, because the correct start is the position of attention, with arms at their sides. Drill sergeants would try to trip us up like that and, needless to say, some of our PT sessions lasted for hours. I did the same thing with my students, except it kept the class fun and interesting, for them and me, unlike basic training. The students had to pay attention and they had a lot of fun. Too bad teachers of classes like English, History, and Science couldn't do the same kind of thing.

A couple weeks into the course, we had a session in which we were told of various qualification training. Airborne School, which is the training for paratroopers, was one option that was offered. It would follow AIT. It sounded like fun, but would add an extra year to my enlistment, so that was the end of that.

We also did a bunch of paperwork, some of which made sense – like insurance forms – and some didn't – like the statements of personal history, which listed every place I had lived.

One duty that was practiced throughout the army was called "fire guard." This was taking turns throughout the night being awake for an hour to watch out for a fire breaking out in the barracks. The fire guard's job would be to sound the alarm and wake up the other soldiers to keep them from dying in their sleep. Each fire guard would wake up the next one before going back to sleep. Sometimes, the next person wasn't fully awake and we'd end up with no one on fire guard. If the drill sergeants discovered this on their periodic checks, we'd all be woken up and screamed at. I don't know if any fires ever broke out anywhere in the army and if the practice of fire guard saved any lives. It just seemed like another way to harass us.

Toward the end of basic, the training got to be more interesting and relevant. One night was taken up by night infiltration training, which involved low crawling across terrain at night while live rounds were fired over us. There was a lot of emphasis placed on not stand-ing up. None of us needed to be reminded.

We also went through nighttime escape and evasion training to prepare us for escaping from captivity, in case we were taken prisoner by the Vietcong – training we hopefully wouldn't ever need.

At the end of basic, you are usually given a leave to go home before your next assignment. This is something we all looked for-ward to even more than just finishing basic. However, there was no leave given, because of the timing of when basic ended and the next Infantry AIT course began, just a couple days between the two. Those of us who were assigned to Infantry AIT were bused to Fort Polk, a 900-mile drive in rickety army buses, about a 20-hour ride. Fortunately, one benefit of basic was that we had all learned to sleep under any conditions, which is what we did for most of the drive.

Beth wasn't able to visit me at Fort Polk, as she did one weekend at Fort Bliss, but we talked on the phone every so many days, at least once a week.

I was at Fort Polk for November, December, and January. The buses arrived at 2:00 in the morning. We got off the bus, exhausted and sleepy, and were immediately put in formation. A captain came out and informed us that "every swinging dick was going to Vietnam." My thought process was "not me." I believed that, some way, I was going to find a way to get out of it. Turns out, he was right and I was wrong.

I was selected from basic to go to the two-week LPC (Leader Preparation Course), which is a leadership school for recruits the basic training drill sergeants identified as having leadership qualities. In my case, it may have been just that I was five or six years older than most of the other trainees. LPC was also at Fort Polk, but at a different location than Tigerland, where Infantry AIT was conducted. It consisted of two weeks where we were taught leadership skills.

I had two friends at AIT, Don Hudson and Ron Lewis. I don't remember if I knew Don from basic, but I think I did. Ron and I went through basic, leadership school, and AIT together. On Friday, November 4, I was with Ron Lewis and we got to meet astronauts James McDivitt and Ed White of the Gemini 4 mission in 1965. McDivitt had been the mission commander and White performed the first U.S. spacewalk. I can't remember where we met them, but I'm sure it was on base and I don't know what they were doing there, but probably some event that we weren't invited to attend, but we got to meet them anyway. Tragically, White died in the Apollo 1 fire on January 27, 1967. McDivitt went on to command Apollo 9, the first flight of the full Apollo spacecraft, which was in 1969.

The next night, we went to a bar on base. It was our first chance to unwind and relax after finishing basic training. However, our relaxing was interrupted when a fight broke out. This was not uncommon in on-base or off-base bars at that time. Young men crowding together and drinking after a stressful day, with the prospect of war looming over them – this was all the ingredients needed for a fight to erupt. If a Black fought a Black or a White fought a White, that was all right. But if a Black and a White fought, all the Blacks would jump in and then all the Whites would join the melee. Furniture would be added to the mix and we'd get hit with chairs and tables, as well as pool cue sticks and anything else that was handy. The MPs would always quickly appear and break it up.

This was in 1966 at probably the height of the civil rights movement here in their town. On base, the Blacks pretty well stay with themselves and the Whites generally stayed among themselves. Still, fights occasionally broke out.

Similar to basic, LPC included lots of inspections and quantifying more weapons – the .45 caliber handgun, .50 cal machine gun (also known as the M2 Browning), and the M16 again. Apparently, the army really wanted us to be proficient with the M16, the primary weapon for most soldiers.

One memorable part of LPC was when we were given a fire-power demonstration. We were put into bleachers at a firing range out in the country, a big open space where they'd cut down all the trees and everything, where we were awed at what we saw. The demonstration started with a sergeant, I believe, with a .45 pistol fired at an ax with the blade pointing at the shooter. On either side of the ax were two balloons. The shooter fired at the ax, where the bullet was split in two, bursting the two balloons. Then, rifles and machine guns were fired at cardboard dummies set up at various distances. This was followed by increasingly larger weapon systems firing downrange – mortars, tanks, artillery pieces. Finally, they showed us a nuclear gun mounted on a Jeep. (They didn't shoot that one.) It was quite a demonstration. They showed us the entire range of weapons the army had at its disposal, from a pistol to a nuclear rocket – all the degrees of power the army had at the time.

The scary drill that I never wrote home about. You'll know why in a minute. We were in a room with a small stage in front and a sergeant was on it lecturing us on something. All of a sudden, a captain burst into the room accompanied by other officers. He threw the sergeant off the stage and in a very angry voice informed us that China had invaded Vietnam. The base was now closed, all mail would be censored, and no phone calls would be allowed. We had three days to get ready to be shipped to Vietnam. We were hustled to the armory and issued our guns, loaded on trucks, and driven out to the field, some training area on base. We went through maneuver exercises, including an ambush where we were shot at (with blanks). It lasted all day. At the end of the day, they brought us back from the field and marched us into the same room. We were exhausted. The captain then informed us that everything that had happened that day was just a drill, an exercise to see how we would react. We were ordered not to mention this exercise to anyone, as each group that passed through this leadership school would be put through the same drill. It scared us to death, but at the end of the day, we were so tired we didn't care. It was kind of a crazy style of training, but I guess we learned something from it and might be somehow more prepared for actual war. It made the idea of combat more real, not just conceptual.

When we completed LPC and received our certificate of training, we were sent to a platoon of new soldiers at AIT, just out of basic training. I was appointed to the position of platoon sergeant and had my own room in the barracks, rather than being in the open bay of bunk beds with the rest of the platoon. We all would go through AIT together, but I received a few benefits for being in a supervisory position. It didn't come with a huge amount of additional responsibility, so I considered it a fair trade.

Each job in the army has its own Advanced Individual Training after basic training, where the soldiers were trained in the specific skills associated with that job. In my case, it was Infantry AIT, so it felt a lot like a continuation of basic training. The various AITs were different lengths, depending on the complexity of the skills which had to be taught. Infantry was one of the shorter ones at about two months, plus a Christmas break. AIT for medic jobs could be as long as a year. Heck, the war might be over by the time they finished training.

On one of the first days of AIT, I saw a bazooka and LAW live-fire demonstration. The bazooka was technically an M79 grenade launcher, which looked like a shotgun and made a "bloop" sound when fired – and a boom sound when the grenade landed. LAW stands for light antitank weapon. It's a short, shoulder-fired rocket-launcher that was used to destroy hardened targets, like tanks or bunkers. It was like a small bazooka.

December 2 was payday and I received $38. Ron Lewis and I went out for a beer. That's the kind of little pleasure in the army that is worth highlighting in a letter home.

We were notified that we were to have a two-week Christmas leave, because this might be the last Christmas we may have. That wasn't a very happy thought. Easy for AIT instructors to say, since they weren't headed off to war. Six of us rented a cab to Dallas, where I caught a plane to Lubbock and they flew wherever their homes were. The cab cost us $25 each, which was cheaper than other travel options, despite the 300-mile drive. Beth picked me up in Lubbock and took me the 100 miles to Clovis. I spent the two weeks with Beth and we went to the cabin in the mountains where we spent our honeymoon. It's hard to describe the two weeks. There were just so many happy moments spent with her and family again. After being apart for so long, each day spent doing something uncomfortable with the war looming over my head, being together with no other concerns was an absolutely good time.

After returning to Fort Polk in January, I had to have a power of attorney and last will made out, even though we had done some of that in basic. The army seemed to be big on duplication of effort and inefficiency. That's their way of making sure it gets done.

The rest of AIT mostly consisted of more Infantry training. We did a 20-mile march with several days on bivouac. It was the middle of January and it rained a lot and was very cold. I can remember the humidity was so high it was as cold as I've been. We passed a PT test, survival test, and an escape and evasion course.

The escape and evasion course was set up with a lot of soldiers trying to capture us and take us to a compound, where they poured chicken blood on us and slap us around a little bit. The compound was in the middle of the course, so we could see a lot of it happening from where we were hiding. These other soldiers played the opposing force in this training all the time, so they knew every place where we might hide or sneak around. In that way, it was similar to trying to escape from enemy territory. The deck was stacked against us from the start. Still, four of us stayed together, managed to get through the course without being caught. I don't know if we were lucky or skilled, but we did it. We kept hidden and low and on the move until the end of the exercise. Somehow, that worked.

Toward the end, we went to Peason Ridge, where we camped out for a week, ate C rations, and were taught how to kill a chicken and eat it. And I don't really remember that, but that's what I wrote home to Beth, so I imagine we did it. This was a place that was set up like a village in Vietnam. We were taught how to search houses, we called them hooches, and otherwise interact with the locals. I was really impressed and thought we had learned a lot about Vietnam. Once I was over there, I realized it wasn't anything like Vietnam. It's crazy to me that, with all the soldiers who had been in-country already, they couldn't create more realistic training.

We also had to go through a night compass course where we each had to use the compass to navigate individually for specific distances on precise azimuths to the finish line. Each of us had learned our individual pace count, that is, how many steps it took us to go 100 meters. We would use the compass to keep us going in the right direction – the compass arrow and numbers glowed in the dark – counting our steps so we knew how far we had traveled. After reaching the first spot, we had to move along different azimuth for another distance, and so on until we successfully reach the end point. It's pretty simple, in concept, and most of us were able to complete the task successfully.

The last thing in AIT was the gas chamber training. We were marched into the gas chamber, which was a large canvas tent, wearing gas masks. Then the tent was filled with tear gas and we were told to take off our masks and count to 10. If the trainers saw that any of us were able to go that long without inhaling, they'd wait until we did. There was no outsmarting them, although we all tried. The tear gas burned our lungs and eyes and made us cough. Once we had all suffered a sufficient amount, we were led back outside and told to put our masks back on. Needless to say, it was not very enjoyable.

I had a 30 day leave after AIT before I left for Vietnam. I spent it at home with Beth. Like the Christmas leave, it was wonderful to have time with her and we made the most of it. Unlike the Christmas leave, we knew I'd be leaving for a year and we didn't know for sure if I'd come back. But we tried not to think about that and just enjoy our time together. Beth is a strong, brave woman and kept her worries to herself. I did the same.

When it was time for me to leave, my brother-in-law, who was a pilot in the Air Force, got me a flight out of Cannon Air Force Base, which is just outside of Clovis. Beth, Mom, and Dad went to see me off. We went to Cannon and I check in for the flight, dropping off my duffle bag for loading onto the plane. Soldiers don't use suitcases, we just crammed everything into a canvas bag with two shoulder straps. It was about 3 feet tall and maybe 20 inches wide. Not much room to pack belongings for a year. Anyway, after checking in, we went to the airport lounge and had a beer. We were looking out the window and a plane took off. Somebody told me, "That's your plane," which meant I missed it. Not the best start to my tour.

My family rushed me to Clovis Airport, which is on the other side of town, got a plane to Lubbock, then to Oakland, California. From there, I caught a bus to Edwards Air Force Base, retrieved my luggage, got back on the bus to return to Oakland for my flight to Vietnam two days later. The trip to Vietnam took 20 hours on a Boeing 707 via Honolulu, Guam, and Okinawa. At least we had an inflight movie and good food, which is more than most flights in the U.S. back then or even now, as I write this book.

Now, I'll get back to the story of my time in the war, picking up with the big battle of March 20.

# CHAPTER 4

LESS THAN A month in country, I lived through a horrific battle. Two of our people were killed and at least 30 were wounded and had to be evacuated. In the aftermath, if I remember accurately, several of our men would be awarded Bronze Stars for Valor, four received Silver Stars – including me – and our medic, Specialist Four Charles Hagemeister, would be presented a Medal of Honor by President Lyndon Johnson.

The citation from my Silver Star award order described my actions in battle with these formal words:

"For gallantry in action: Private First Class Hoy distinguished himself by exceptionally valorous action on 20 March 1967, while serving as a rifleman with Company A, 1st Battalion, 5th Cavalry during an engagement with a numerically superior enemy force in the village of Tan An, Republic of Vietnam. As Private First Class Hoy's company moved to set up a blocking position, it received heavy enemy small arms and automatic weapons fire from the village and a treeline. Finding himself in an exposed position affording an excellent opportunity to engage the enemy, Private First Class Hoy immediately returned a heavy volume of fire, killing several of the enemy soldiers to his front. Upon learning that friendly casualties nearby were pinned down and badly in need of assistance, Private First Class Hoy, with complete disregard for his own safety moved forward to an even more exposed position, increasing his suppressive fire on the hostile force to enable other members of his platoon to render assistance to the wounded. Private First Class Hoy's action contributed significantly to saving several lives. His gallantry under fire is in keeping with the highest traditions of the military service, and reflects great credit upon himself, his unit, and the United States Army."

There was a lot more to the battle than that. Here is what I remember or what I wrote in my letter to Bud, my dad. Also, a VC was captured and this includes the info he gave.

The Vietcong saw us air assault in. It was about 3:30 in the afternoon. They set up an L-shape ambush to get us. This was a fairly typical tactic by the Vietcong and by us. The long side of the L paralleled the anticipated route of travel, often either a trail or a road. The ambushers on that axis shoot from the side. The short part of the L would shoot down the length of the trail or road.

It was my understanding that there was a brigade of VC or North Vietnamese army, about 400 fighters. I don't know if there were 300 or 400, but there were a bunch of them. We were a company under full strength. I believe we had 136 men in our company at the time, far short of the 170 authorized.

The choppers flew us to the Binh Dinh Province and we landed near the village of Tan An, where the captain, our company commander, immediately put us on a line and started marching us toward the village. By this, I mean we were lined up left to right, spread out, not one person in front of the other. I'm sure that the VC had been spotted previously and the captain had been informed.

As always, it was miserably hot and humid and we were carrying 80-pound rucksacks. We did drop the rucks when it was apparent that we needed more agility. Until then, the weight we were carrying in that heat was insufferable – on top of the fact that a lot of bad guys were soon trying to kill us.

Women and children emerged from the village and walked toward us. They normally don't come out and meet you. We put them in front of us and marched them back toward the village. The only male was the old papasan with a white beard and long white hair, dressed in black pants and shirt. We called them "pajamas," because of their loose fit. He refused to go back to the village. I was told by my squad leader to make him go. So, I tried pushing him forward, but that didn't work and he dropped to the ground. I then grabbed him by the hair and dragged him. After about 25 yards, I had enough and dropped him, so I could keep up with my squad. He wasn't doing us any good, anyway. Turns out, he was a smart papasan. He knew what was waiting for us ahead.

The women and children were clearly nervous and didn't want to be where they found themselves, between us and the enemy. The enemy, who was hiding in the village, opened up firing and all hell broke loose. We were immediately pinned down in an open area. My location was in the middle of a graveyard. I was on the left-hand side of the line. This graveyard was not full of headstones, like American cemeteries. They were just little mountains of dirt, probably no more than two feet high. That was better than nothing, better than a flat area with nothing to duck behind. We dropped down behind the mounds of dirt and started to return fire from the sides of the mounds or over the tops of them.

There was a lieutenant just to the right of me. Behind him was his radio operator. The lieutenant looked over the top to see what was happening and got shot in the head. His radio operator was behind him and when I looked over, I saw that he was crying. I don't know if he was crying about the lieutenant or from fear for himself. I told him if he didn't start firing his weapon, I would shoot him myself. Maybe that was a little harsh and just my reaction to the moment. We are all affected in different ways.

I later learned that the lieutenant had just been promoted to captain and only had one day left in the country. He had heard that there would be a battle and he wanted one more firefight, so he volunteered to come out and join us. He had been assigned to our unit earlier in his tour, but officers were rotated to the rear after six months in country. Before leaving Vietnam, he wanted to be in one more fight with his unit, so there he was. Sadly, he would never pin on his captain bars. The guy with one day left who wanted one more firefight got shot in the head and died. Looking back, I get what he felt. I understand what it's like to want one more fight. Battle was the height of competition in my life, something I haven't experienced since then and never will again.

About 75 to 100 yards in front of me was a two-man machine gun position firing on us – one man is the shooter and the other keeps feeding ammunition into the weapon. These were the ones who shot the lieutenant in the head. One hundred yards isn't very far away for a machine gun, especially if you're on the receiving end. Dirt was kicking up all around me and I couldn't figure out what it was at first, in all the noise and confusion. It was bullets from machine gun. There were three or four soldiers to my left pinned down behind the graves. We were pinned down for two hours, returning fire. Combat doesn't always happen as quickly as you see in the movies. Two hours is a long time to be shot at and pinned down behind a small mound of dirt, not really knowing what's going on.

Someone threw a smoke grenade – it was purple – to mark the front of our position, so a helicopter could come in and start firing. The guy who threw the smoke grenade was behind us, so most of us were in front of the smoke. In other words, we were in front of where the helicopter thought we were, in the area where the pilot thought there was only VC. The helicopter came in real low with both door gunners firing M60 machine guns. One of our sergeants ran out and yelled at them, trying to alert the door gunners that they were shooting at some of our soldiers. Finally. the chopper flew away, luckily before they killed or wounded any of us. It's bad enough dealing with the threat on the ground to our front, without having to worry about a threat from our own air support.

In my letter, I said the enemy was sneaking up and throwing grenades at us and the civilians who were still curled up, trembling in fear, in front of us. We threw grenades back at the enemy, along with shooting at them when we were able to line up a good shot. Wasting our bullets just to shoot wildly wasn't smart. Grenades had a wider kill radius than bullets, although we didn't have an unlimited supply of those either. Between myself and the soldiers around me, we were finally able to shoot the two guys manning the machine gun, which took some of the pressure off. There were still a lot of other enemy soldiers trying to kill us, though.

After a while, both of our machine gunners were wounded or killed, and we were putting other people on those weapons. M60 machine guns were much more effective than our M16s at killing or suppressing the Vietcong, so we had to keep them manned – and the

VC kept firing at that position. Three other guys in our fire squad were hit.

We saw the enemy trying to flank us on our left. My sergeant and I got up and went to repel them. By using a fire and maneuver method – one man shoots as the other moves forward to another position, taking turns to leapfrog ahead – we managed to get behind them and took care of them, killing a few and scaring off the others. Another soldier who had taken over the machine gun from the wounded soldier joined us.

We found a spot that gave us a vantage point with a view over much of the area, so we could cover both the left flank and any advances from the village. It left us a little exposed from those directions, though, too. So, we had to stay constantly alert for the next few hours, as the enemy saw that we were more vulnerable and we repeatedly had to repel them. While we were shielding our buddies from attacks on that side, we were too far away from them by now for them to effectively cover us. It got a little lonely out there for the three of us, but we hung in there and did some damage to the enemy.

By this time, it had grown dark, although it remained hot. The hooches were on fire and there were flares being dropped, which gave us some light to see by. The VC could also see a little better by this light, but the flares are generally fired away from us and toward the enemy, giving us the advantage.

At one point early on, there was a group of VC running in front of the burning hooches and I began to fire at them. I yelled at the machine gunner to start shooting.

He replied, "Where are they? I can't see them."

I looked at him and I said, "Take off those goddamn sunglasses."

He had forgotten that he was wearing sunglasses as the light of day had faded. He said, "Oh shit," took off the sunglasses, and got back into the fight, firing at the running VC that he could now see.

A lot of stuff in war is funny like that, even in the middle of a battle. It may seem hard to imagine, but most soldiers will tell you it's true. Some of it is funny at the time and other stuff is funny looking back on it. Yes, there are terrible things that happen and I wouldn't minimize or detract from the horrors that men and women experience in war. Still, my wartime experience included many humorous moments, some of which I've included in this book. That reality is one thing I want to communicate clearly. War is not all hell all the time. There is a great deal of laughter and ridiculousness, even at the worst of times.

At about 9:30 that night, we were still somewhat separated from the rest of the company, having moved off to the left, pursuing the VC and then moved forward toward the village. Another soldier got to us and said we should pull back. There were Vietcong crawling up on us. I told the others I would throw a grenade and, when it goes off, we would run. It wasn't a perfect plan, because we didn't know exactly where the enemy was or if the grenade would hit them. We also didn't know if the VC who were outside the blast radius would see us running and start firing at us. It was the best plan we had, though. I tossed the grenade, it blew up, and the four of us took off, with the soldier who had come to get us leading us back to the rest of the company.

We didn't realize how far separated from the company we now were and that they had flown in another company and set up a security perimeter behind us. Our company had withdrawn there, except for us. I was the last person to get back within the perimeter. A sergeant came by and asked if we needed anything. I told him a drink of water was what I needed most, having spent many hours fighting in the Vietnam heat. My canteens were long empty and my mouth was parched. He gave me his canteen and, boy, did it taste good.

Once we were back in the perimeter, the commander called in Puff the Magic Dragon. This is a C-130 airplane with three 7.62 mm Gatling guns, all on the pilot's side, the left side. Firing at a rate of 2,000 rounds per minute, it places one round every 2½ yards over a 50-yard diameter area during a three-second burst. Every fifth round is a tracer, which burns brightly, so the shooter can see where it's going and make any necessary adjustments. When it flew over and started firing, it looked like a red arm came down from the black sky and swept the area. It was quite a sight.

There were helicopters coming in and taking off, flying out the wounded, bringing in supplies. There was a lot of stuff going on.

When we had moved to the left and I left my pack behind that grave. I took all my ammo plus 200 rounds from the lieutenant who was shot and his grenades. For some reason, things ran in sevens. We fought for seven hours. I fired 700 rounds, threw seven grenades, and when we got back, I had seven rounds left. Maybe seven is my lucky number. It was that day, anyway.

The three of us – my sergeant, the machine gunner, and me – dug a foxhole that night with our steel pots (helmets). Our entrenching tools (shovels) were with our packs which we had left behind us. That night, while digging our foxhole, I lost my wedding ring. My fingers had gotten thinner, because of all the physical exertion and the water weight lost from sweating. The ring just slipped off and was lost in the dirt as we dug. I was disappointed when I realized it was missing, but couldn't find it.

As we sat in the foxhole, we were able to decompress a little and take stock of what had happened. The sergeant I was with had gotten hit on the arm by shrapnel. The next day I looked at my helmet and saw where it had been scratched by shrapnel in three different places. Those are pretty close calls. A few inches lower and I might have joined the lieutenant.

Our platoon started with 28 men and, after it was all over with, we were left with only 19. Of the casualties, only two were killed. No one else was killed in the other platoons, but they did have some wounded. That is what I wrote to Bud, anyway. I can't remember the exact number killed or wounded in our company. I just know that from 136, they only had 30-something in the field the next day. At least, that's what I remember and it might not be accurate. In all honesty, it was probably more like 30 injured and 2 killed, leaving us about 100 the next day.

During the battle, I wasn't afraid. I found that the fear wouldn't hit me until the next day. Maybe this was a defense mechanism, my mind's way of keeping me focused on the task at hand, staying alive. If I started crying like that radio operator, I couldn't do what had to be done, couldn't return fire and maneuver against the enemy. Whatever the reason, that's the way it was for me throughout the war. Like I said before, everyone is affected in different ways. My way isn't the right way or a better way and it's not something I chose, but I'm fortunate that it's how my brain responded to the danger.

The next day, the company that came out to help us moved out and tried to follow and locate the VC. Our company moved out and dragged in the dead VC and took over the battlefield. The women and children who had been in front of us during the battle were all dead, except for two babies the mothers had laid on top of to protect, I wrote to Dad that they had been killed by hand grenades, but that was wrong. From what we could tell by the amount of damage to them, they were shot by Puff the Magic Dragon. It's hard to describe how mutilated the bodies of the civilians were. You could see right through them, rib cages, internal organs, and all. I can't say for sure how much of this was from bullets, grenades, or the gunship, but no one survived Puff. I know that there are still things I'll always remember.

In my letter, I said that there were two of us up for Silver Stars and six for Bronze Stars. Our medic, Specialist Five Chuck Hagemeister, was up for the Medal of Honor, which is the highest award in the military. The Silver Star is the third highest, after the Distinguished Service Cross, and the Bronze Star follows next. If I remember right, four were eventually awarded Silver Stars, including SP5 Hagemeister. After he was later awarded the Medal of Honor, it replaced the Silver Star he had previously received. I don't know how many were awarded Bronze Stars.

I didn't hear about what Hagemeister had done to earn the Medal of Honor until later, second or third-hand. He tended to the wounded at the machine gun position near me on the left flank, along with many other casualties, crawling from one to the next under heavy fire for hours. Our platoon leader, a lieutenant, got shot by a sniper and Hagemeister bandaged him while the sniper continued to fire at them. The medic laid across the lieutenant at one point to shield him and then was able to shoot back, killing the sniper. He repeatedly retrieved wounded soldiers who were in exposed areas to the front of our company's position and returned fire, killing a number of the enemy. When the company pulled back into the secure perimeter, Hagemeister ensured that no wounded were left behind to our front, again putting himself in great danger. Because of him choosing to risk his own life, many of our soldiers survived. Happily, so did he.

We had killed 53 Vietcong and wounded 20. One of them was a brigade commander. They were part of the Yellow Star Division, which is a crack outfit of the PAVN, People's Army of Vietnam. (The PAVN is the same as the NVA, North Vietnamese Army.) All of this information is according to the captured VC.

When we were pulled out of the area, we went back to An Khe and were sent on less threatening missions, if there is such a thing. I later realized this is how the army works. If you have been in a major battle and lost a large number of men to casualties, it takes a while to find enough soldiers to bring the unit back up to strength. We were never actually up to full strength that an infantry company is supposed to have, but we eventually got back up to having enough manpower to be combat ready. During this time of remanning, they put us in areas that are not considered to be as dangerous as other areas, so we could recuperate.

Our recuperation started with being back at An Khe for a small Easter celebration and with some good news for the unit.

# CHAPTER 5

ON EASTER WEEKEND, I had been there one month with eleven to go. The first month had gone by quickly, but looking ahead at the next eleven felt like a long way to go, especially after the big battle we had just gone through. I hoped every month didn't include an experience like that.

Happy Easter! Being Easter Sunday, I put on my best fatigues (uniform) – the only ones I have – and my camouflage helmet, and go Easter VC hunting, with my little M16 Easter basket. Not much happening today. We climbed a tall mountain, in the miserable heat, as always. Up there, we were told that the whole company was up for the Presidential Unit Citation, an important honor. If we get it, we would be the first company to be awarded it during the Vietnam War. As it stands, with the individual medals, we would be the most decorated company for battle in Vietnam. I don't know if that is true or not, but we were told by the Colonel that we did the best job during a firefight that he had ever seen. We were interviewed by newsmen and photographers took pictures of us. Talk for about a year. I then interviewed and made reports about what happened and still don't know what we did that was so great. It seems like the same thing we did in the other battles.

That afternoon on top of the mountain, I was awarded the Silver Star for what I had done in the big battle a few days earlier. Personally, I think I received the medal more for where I was than for what I had done. I don't feel like I really did anything so special, but it was in the worst part of the battle with two other guys, kind of removed from the rest of the company by a short distance.

The presentation was performed out in the field. We were camped on the mountaintop and all the big brass was flown out, including Major General (two-star) Norton, commanding general of the 1st Air Calvary Division. There were also more officers and high-ranking NCOs than I had ever seen in the field before. It was a pretty big deal. Four of us were presented Silver Stars and four others received Bronze Stars. As I mentioned earlier, this was an interim award for our medic, while his Medal of Honor nomination was processed. The same was true for our sergeant, who was put in for a Distinguished Service Cross. I don't know if the sergeant ever got that upgrade.

During the ceremony, it was raining and we were all standing at attention. The weather doesn't take orders from a general. The general stood at attention on front of each of us as our award orders were read. He would then pin the medal on our uniform shirt. I had been growing a mustache since arriving in Vietnam, as mentioned earlier, and it had gotten pretty big. With the rain, it was hanging down in my mouth. The general was standing in front of me – my boss's boss's boss's boss's boss' boss – and I looked like a ragbag. I was really embarrassed. This was the first time I personally met a general, much less my division commander. Plus, he was there to honor me, to present me my first military award. And, here I was, looking like Private Sad Sack. I didn't want to know what he was thinking, nor what all the bosses between me and him in the command structure were thinking. I made a promise to myself right then to never be in such a humiliating situation again. Right after this award business was over, I would shave that thing off my face. And, I did. Besides that, it was nice to be recognized for my actions, even if I didn't feel like it was anything worth making a big deal out of. We had all just done our jobs, what we had been trained to do.

I wrote to Beth that we had made five air assaults already and it was really something to ride on these helicopters. That shows you how new I was. You eventually can't remember how many air assaults you had made. At the end of my tour, I was awarded an Air Medal for making 25 air assaults. If you made 50, you got an oak leaf cluster on the medal. To get that, though, you had to have the pilots sign off on every mission. I didn't really have time for that kind of paperwork as we were landing at an LZ (landing zone). It seemed more important at those moments to just jump out and get going on the mission before anyone started shooting at us. Can you imagine a squad of soldiers handing the pilot their logbooks on the LZ and asking for signatures before hopping off the chopper? It was a ridiculous bit of bureaucracy. I probably made 100 air assaults during my full time in Vietnam. I didn't get a single signature from the pilots.

During a helicopter insertion, each squad was in one UH-1 "Huey" helicopter, some sitting in the open doors. As the helicopters set down, we would hop out of each side and the bird would immediately lift off again. For a platoon insertion, usually four helicopters were used. If the LZ was big enough, all four would land at once, only far enough apart to keep their rotor blades from hitting each other. It was a very quick way to get a unit on the ground. I liked it a lot more than hiking many miles up and down mountains.

I don't want to sound like a preacher, but every night before I go to bed, I say a prayer. It really helps. I feel like I can really communicate with Him. I have so much to be thankful for and thought it was time I started thanking The Man for them. I don't ask for much, not for myself, anyway. It's more about being grateful for what I have. They say there are no atheists in foxholes and I'm starting to understand why. It's not that I've completely changed my religious attitude. It's been more of a subtle change in my attitude about life. I will have more to say about talking to God later.

On March 28, my rifle squad was flown to a mountain top to be observers for a few days. Observation missions are great for me to catch up on my letter writing. They pick us up in a chopper and have that chopper land on quite a few mountains. When they get to the spot where they want us to set up, we get off. The reason they land at a bunch of locations before and after we get off, which is called "false insertions," is so the VC won't know which one was actually where we dismounted. Once we're on the ground, we dig foxholes and take turns watching for any enemy movement. If we spot anyone, we radio in their location. This could result in a ground unit moving there to engage, or an artillery or gunship attack, or often nothing came of it and it was presumably added to the ton of information that the military intelligence people tracked. The important thing for us is that we don't give away our location by being seen. Another way we might give away our location – and this is a little tricky – is if multiple targets around us get hit by artillery or other attacks while we were there. From those attacks, the enemy could figure out where the observers are sitting and watching and try to take us out. That's one reason why we only stay in one spot for a short time, a few days at most. We sat up there for two days and didn't see much. I'm not sure how they pick the spots for us to observe from, if it's where they expect us to see enemy activity or it's where friendly troops will be inserted soon.

After those couple days, the helicopters came back and flew us to rejoin the company. It had been really hot on the mountain and we ran out of water, so it was a huge relief to see those birds fly in to get us. It might seem easy to take enough water along, but when it's as hot as it was those two days, we just sweat more and went through a lot more water.

Back with the company, I learned that I had been put in for promotion to Specialist 4th Class, what used to be called Corporal. It's the rank just below Sergeant and above Private First Class. It's the fourth enlisted rank. What was important to me is the pay raise that went with it, $49 a month – up to $177.90 from $128.70. It was the biggest pay jump between the enlisted ranks, at least until you got to the two couple levels. The other nice thing was to not be called "Private" or "PFC" anymore. "Specialist" sounds a lot better. I wouldn't know if I got the promotion for a while. I appreciated that my sergeant and lieutenant put me in for it. Speaking of pay, today was payday. I got $50 and the rest was sent home to Beth.

Yesterday, four guys from another platoon got hit by a booby trap. One was killed and three were injured. The one that was killed was one of the replacements that had arrived with me a little over a month ago. We were already short of men from the big battle and would need more replacements soon. I hope that doesn't sound cold. It's just the reality. When a unit lost soldiers through death or injury, it was left weaker and incapable of performing its mission as effectively. We'd still get sent out on missions, though, and would be at greater risk. So, we all wanted to get more replacements in quickly.

I went on a long-range patrol with seven other guys. Our job was just observation, not engagement. My letter to Beth didn't mention us running into any Vietcong.

On April 4, our area of operation was changed from the mountains to the lowlands. My legs were happy to not have to climb up and down all day. In the lowlands, we went from village to village, looking for Vietcong and weapons caches. We captured a few VC. Usually, we'd go through a village and see no males, except maybe an old papasan. When we did find males, we'd capture them and send them to the rear to be interrogated. In these hostile areas, we knew that everyone was either actively fighting as Vietcong or sympathetic to them and providing some kind of support – hiding places, food, lodging, storage for their weapons and ammunition, things like that. I don't know what was done with them after they were interrogated, probably kept in prisoner of war camps.

We once had a man missing and found him with his fingers cut off and burned to death in a haystack. The lieutenant that was killed during the firefight had supposedly scalped a VC earlier in his tour in retaliation for things the VC did, like burning this man. What the lieutenant did was a cruel, horrible thing to do and I can't defend him doing that, but I can see how a person could get that way after seeing what the Vietcong often did to our soldiers. Sometimes, our side punished people who committed offenses like what the lieutenant did. More often, nothing was done to them. In any case, I know for sure that the Vietcong didn't punish their people for illegal and inhumane acts.

If we got sniper fire from a village, we burned it down. On the other hand, sometimes we received a friendly welcome from villagers who were happy to see us, maybe those who didn't like the Vietcong or were on neither side. The children might run up to us and say, "G.I. number one, give chop-chop." I'm not sure, but I think "chop-chop" meant food. The villagers would cut down a coconut and give it to us. We would give them chewing gum and cigarettes, both of which we got in every C-ration box. Everyone smoked in the villages, even the little kids. There was one kid who had big eyes and was really a cute kid. It's hard to say how old he was, but very young anyway. I kept trying to make him come to me, so I could give him some gum. He wanted the gum, but was scared to come to me. So, I walked over to give it to him and he started to cry. His mother got a big kick out of the whole scene and seemed to be telling him to stop crying, as she laughed. I gave him the gum and stepped back away. He took it and stopped crying. I can't blame him for being scared of me, as I hadn't shaved in four days and probably looked pretty scary.

Late at night on April 4, it got kind of spooky. After days of patrolling villages, we had stopped for the night, dug foxholes, and were taking turns sleeping. I was able to take my boots off for the first time in a week, which was a huge relief. Not long after I feel asleep, the VC dropped mortars on us. The three of us jumped into the foxhole really quickly. Trying to put my shoes back on in a foxhole with two other guys was a tight squeeze. The shelling went on most of the night. The good news was that they didn't seem to know exactly where we were or didn't have spotters advising the guns how to adjust fire to hit us. That was little comfort, though, as explosions continued, some farther some closer. We never knew if one was going to drop right in our foxhole. I guess if one did, we'd still never know it.

We heard rumors out there in the field that we'd be going back to An Khe on April 11, in just under a week. In the meantime, we would be airlifted to LZ English to guard it. This would mean showers, rest, and beer. I talked a lot in my letters about LZ English, so we must have gone there pretty often or received a lot of support from there. It was a helicopter base and pretty safe, about two miles north and a little east of Bong Son. It's definitely safer than patrolling from village to village and taking mortar fire through the night. We did take a little mortar fire one night, but not much and no one got hurt.

This was a larger base, about 5 square miles. One of the reasons for its size was the runway. I'm not sure why helicopters need a runway, but they used it. The base also had a lot of semi-permanent buildings. I think some of 1st Cav's headquarters elements were based there.

I wrote to Beth that I got a shower at LZ English. That should tell you how dirty and grimy we were most of the time, that taking a shower is "something to write home about." Going a few weeks without a shower wasn't unusual at all. Even having a chance to bathe in a river was a rare treat. At LZ English, our unit also had its own bunker, a steel-roofed building. We kept a garbage can full of ice, where we put our beer, cokes, and fruit. We were living the life of luxury.

Beth had asked in a letter what I wanted her to send me. I asked for little cans of fruit. I received a package from home while at LZ English. It included Mandarin oranges, which I loved. We didn't have much fruit that year and those were delicious. I had also requested packets of Kool-Aid, so she sent me one in each letter. I would put it in my canteen with the water. It tasted great. It was little things like that that made my day over there. It's hard to imagine, if you haven't been in a similar situation, just how much these little things can brighten a soldier's day. Actually, every letter from home made my day. It's funny how, although I knew Beth was writing to me every day, the days when I didn't receive one, it was a letdown. I knew that the military postal system wasn't the most efficient or consistent and that I might receive three letters one day and none for three days – on April 12, I received six letters, a great day! For this reason, I knew rationally that getting no mail didn't mean Beth hadn't written to me, it just meant that the letter was en route. But, being handed a letter from home made me happy. Not receiving one made me a little sad. I'd shake it off and quickly forget about it and look forward to a letter the next day.

I've mentioned that there's humor in war. Here's another example. They kicked up the price of beer for the army guys who come to LZ English. They probably did this thinking that it would cut down on our drinking. It didn't. One of the guys I ran around with paid $5 for ten bottles of gook beer, local Vietnamese beer. (I know the term "gook" isn't acceptable anymore, but it's what we said back then and what I wrote in the letters, so I'm using it in this book to reflect the time when I was in Vietnam.) I knew I could beat that. I went to the hospital tent on the base and looked around. The doctors had their own refrigerated van and they keep it well stocked with beer. I just walked up like I owned the place and ordered a case of beer. They asked me where I was from and I replied "15th Medical Corps." I got my case of Budweiser for $3 and took it to the garbage can of ice in our tent. Word got out that we had Budweiser. One of the more senior sergeants who worked at the CP (command post) would radio that he had to talk to us and would be over right away. A few minutes later, he'd show up at our tent, have a beer, and then go back to the CP.

Our second night at LZ English around midnight, someone ran into our bunker and woke us up and told us that two tanks had run out of gas. We had to go out and secure them, that is, provide security for them until fuel could be brought to them. As we were walking down the road in the dark, we ran into some South Vietnamese soldiers. Without any light to see by, there was no way to tell them from North Vietnamese. So, we jumped them, took their weapons, and pushed them around a little period. We scared them pretty good – and they scared us. It's fortunate that none of us started shooting. It could have been an unfortunate friendly fire incident. Once we realized our mistake, we returned their weapons and let them go on their way. We finally found the tanks at around 3:00 in the morning and secured them, setting up a small perimeter.

It turned out that we didn't go back to An Khe, after all. Instead, after just a couple days at LZ English, we were sent to LZ Montezuma, a Marine base about 15 miles north of LZ English and 40 miles north of An Khe, just off the coast. The Marines had been getting a beating and we were sent to help them. There were supposed to be about 2,800 hardcore Vietcong in the area. Our mission was to go out and make contact with them, our usual mission, one that we were getting used to, even if it never sounded like any fun. This time, though, we were able to have a little fun.

We air assaulted onto the beach to protect an amphibious landing operation to bring in more Marines. Once the operation was over, we took the opportunity to go swimming. Even though we had just showered the day before at LZ English, we couldn't pass on the chance to hit the waves. I could now say I had been swimming in the South China Sea. I have never even seen the ocean or a sea until coming to Vietnam. There were big waves, so big that they caused the landing craft to crash onto the shore. When we went swimming, we would ride the waves in, then swim back out, diving under the incoming waves. The waves lifted us high into the air and gently bring us back down – until we caught one the wrong way, dragging us on the bottom, tossing us through somersaults. We didn't have swimsuits, so it kind of made it rough on our backsides. I'll leave it at that.

My letters didn't include any mention of combat. I take this to mean we didn't have any major run ins with the Vietcong. Our movement to contact mission seems to have had much more movement than contact.

Another funny story happened at about this time. Well, the people involved might not have thought it was funny. I bet they're still telling the story today, though. We had been airlifted to a mountaintop on an observation mission. There were several squads doing the same thing in the area. One night, we heard over the radio that one squad had a panther and her two cubs come in on them and start eating their food. The night before, only the momma panther had come to the location and eaten a few C-rations. I guess she liked them more than we did, because she brought her family back a night later. The first night, the squad just got out of her way, but with her cubs along, they were afraid she might attack if she thought her kids were in danger. The squad couldn't shoot the panthers, because it would give away their position to the VC. So, they were asking for advice from the CP. The patrol leader said, "I was taught to fight VC, not pussycats." The ingenious advice they were given was to bark like a dog, as if cats that big would be scared of a dog. I don't know if this was supposed to be a joke or serious, lifesaving advice, but it wasn't much of a solution and the rest of us who were listening got a good laugh. Finally, one of the soldiers took his mosquito repellent off his helmet – remember that we all had to carry mosquito repellent on our helmets? – and squirted the panthers with it. This did the trick and the cats ran off and didn't come back. They must have thought C-rations weren't worth a faceful of bug spray. Because the patrol happened to have a reporter embedded with them, the story got back to the States and was printed in the New York Times. I used to have a copy of it and probably still do.

Also on that mission, we were given LRPs, Long Range Patrol rations. They were dehydrated food in a plastic bag. We'd heat up water with our heat tablets – which got hot, but didn't produce a flame – and pour the water into the plastic bag and stir. Presto! Instant hot meals. And, they were really great. As I said, we can't give away our position by lighting fires to heat the water, but the heat tablets did the trick. A hot meal is wonderful for morale when you're in the field.

Back from the observation mission, I went four days without any mail. I was feeling pretty blue about that. Then, on April 17, I received seven letters! This changed my mood 180 degrees for the better.

When I got back from Vietnam, I would tell people that I only saw the base camp at An Khe three times. But that had to be wrong. As I reread my letters to prepare for this book, I saw that I was there more often than that. For example, I had completely forgotten about going there for a five-day leadership school with another soldier. We had been chosen by the captain, our company commander, to attend. I don't know if I cared that much about the training, but it was nice to be out of the field for a while.

The other big benefit was that I could make a phone call to the States. I tried to call Beth, but she wasn't home. I learned later that she had gone to Alamogordo. I gave the operator another phone number and got to talk to Mom and Dad. It was nice to hear their voices and they were thrilled to hear from me and know I was safe. These calls were transmitted by radio from An Khe to a fort in California for free. This was by Military Auxiliary Radio System (MARS). From there, the call went by normal phone lines and long distance rates to Clovis. It was a radio call, so when you finish speaking, you have to say "over" to let the other party know that it was their turn to talk. I was used to this manner of speaking, but my parents had trouble getting the hang of it.

We were two days late arriving at the leadership course, which wasn't our fault, of course. That was minus 200 points. Our uniforms were dirty and unkempt, which made us stand out from most of the other students. We had missed a test worth 50 points in those two days that we weren't there. So, starting off, we were already down 250 points. You could only lose 300 points and still pass the course. We asked an officer who was an instructor what we could do. He said to come back for the next session of the school. We kind of hid out each day until dark and then went back to the barracks. We've got three days at base camp by doing this, which wasn't bad at all. I had gotten a package from Beth when I was at An Khe that contained a tape and more fruit. Because we were "ditching school," I couldn't get to my tape recorder or pick up my package from Beth or else we would have been caught and sent back to the field. It was the price I paid for getting a little more rest. We rejoined the company two days later. We hadn't learned much about leadership, except maybe to make sure you get your soldiers to schools in time for the start of the course.

After my return to the company, I wrote home about going on patrols, setting up ambushes, and so on. More importantly, I got the package from Beth and a letter with more Kool-Aid. I found that adding it to coconut milk made a delicious drink.

Almost a month had passed since the big battle. I can't say for sure that the company had gotten back up to strength by then, but it seemed that our time of easier, safer missions would eventually come to an end, and probably soon.

# CHAPTER 6

I'VE REPEATEDLY SAID that we went on various missions, but haven't really described what we did, which probably made it a little unclear. So, I'll now discuss a little bit about what we did at night in the field. When I first got first got over to Vietnam, everything was new to me. I don't remember now if what we did and how we did it was the same as later on and, if things changed, I don't remember what order we did things. I was just tickled to be alive and keep going from day to day. Later on, we basically did one of three things. One, we secured the perimeter. Two, a fire squad would be on a listening post (LP). Three, a fire squad would set up an ambush.

Securing the perimeter involves digging foxholes for each three-man team, a line of them around our location. How far apart they were depended on terrain and vegetation. We had to be able to provide the next foxhole supporting fire when needed and also be able to communicate with each other, but spread out far enough to cover as broad an area as possible. This usually meant that we were 10 to 15 yards apart. Each platoon was assigned a portion of the 360-degree perimeter. The area we encircled was maybe 50 to 100 yards across, with the company CP and mortar platoon in the middle, dug into their own foxholes. The mortars would be shot off throughout the night in what was called harassment fire in likely target areas. It kept the VC's heads down and discouraged them from patrolling. It might have even caused a few enemy casualties.

In front of each foxhole, we would set up a trip flare which would light up the area if someone disturbed a wire attached to the flare, usually by catching it with their foot as they walked past. The wire was set up across where we thought any approaching enemy would walk as they approached. The light from the flare would alert us to the enemy and show us where they were, so we could shoot at them. We would also set up a Claymore mine with a wire back to our foxhole. A Claymore mine was a curved device 8 1/2 inches wide, 1 3/8 inches deep, 3 1/4 inches tall, and weighed 3 1/2 pounds. It contained 700 steel ball bearings imbedded in 1 ½ pounds of C-4 plastic explosive. The business side of the mine had the words "Front Toward Enemy" embossed on it in big letters. It seemed kind of funny, but was an important reminder when we were exhausted or sleepy, which was most of the time. When we saw Vietcong to the front of the Claymore, we'd push the trigger and cause a blast that had a range of 50 to 100 yards and an angle of 60 degrees. When we fired the mine, we had to be damn sure we were down in the foxhole, because the backlash could hit us as far as 100 yards back. If not the actual backblast, then secondary shrapnel from the explosion. It was a very handy tool for defending a position.

The listening posts were set up 30 to 50 yards in front of the rest of the platoon. Their job was to provide advanced detection of anyone trying to sneak up on our company. The squad assigned this job would rotate who would sleep and who would listen, because it was very important that the listener remained alert at all times. You didn't want to be the guy who let the VC sneak past you and attack your buddies. When the other squads positioned and aimed their Claymores, they had to be aware of where the LPs were located to keep them out of the blast area.

The third thing we were doing was a fire squad on ambush. We were given a certain destination where we would hide in the jungle, usually in the bushes just off a path or trail, and wait for a patrol of VC to come along. Sometimes, this location would be up to ten clicks (ten kilometers, or about six miles) from where the company was set up. We would put up a trip wire across the trail hooked up to a flare. When the enemy came by and tripped the flare, that was the signal for the squad to open up. The flare was placed near one end of the kill zone, so when their point man tripped it, the rest of the VC patrol would be in our target area. Our squad would be spread out to cover that area with fire. Usually, our machinegun would be at the end of the kill zone, the flare end, shooting down the length of the trail.

So, each night, you were either securing the perimeter, on an LP, or on an ambush. This is how it went from about the middle of my tour to the end of it, almost every night. During the day, we often moved to a new location. The first part of my tour, we may not have done it like this every night. There had been more variation.

When I first arrived, if you were down to 30 days left in country, they would rotate you to the rear in order to start getting you ready to leave the country. By the rear, I mean An Khe, where the 1st Cav was headquartered. This was a lot safer than being out in the field and patrolling every night, so having 30 days in the rear felt like 30 days less of a combat tour. We got a new captain partway through my year and he reduced that to 15 days left in the tour before we could rotate out. Our last captain came in and reduced it to seven days left. I don't understand why they would do this, except maybe to keep the company's strength up. Maybe they were pressured by the higher ups to do it or maybe they thought it made them look more gung ho. Whatever the reason, none of us were happy about the changes.

On April 26, we had been air assaulted to the top of another mountain, where our job for two or three days was to be a radio relay for the other squads going out every day on the usual patrols. This was a good break, because the day before we had been on an all-day patrol and the night before that we were on a night ambush. It had rained all day and off and on all night. We slept in a rice paddy with four inches of water in it. We didn't get much sleep. It was miserable. So, pulling radio relay on a mountaintop for a couple days was heaven in comparison.

I wrote to Beth that we weren't having much enemy contact. We were expecting 20 replacement troops and were waiting for them to arrive before going on any missions where heavy contact was expected. Until then, our patrols were in less hostile areas. On one of these, we camped by a stream that we dammed up to make a swimming pool. That was fun and also got us cleaned up a little. It lifted our spirits.

My captain told me that we would be invading North Vietnam. He told me this like it was really going to happen. He said the Marines would make a landing from the sea and 1st Cav would make a huge air assault to the inland. He said we were getting new recruits in for this purpose and would have them within two weeks and be back to full strength. I knew we never had been at full strength and probably never would. Full strength for us was 160-plus men and we were at about 120, which was still pretty good, considering our past manning levels and the impact of the big battle.

As we know now, that ground attack on North Vietnam never happened. We bombed that country from the air, but didn't send in ground troops. I heard that we didn't want China to enter the war, like it had done in Korea.

That's the bad thing about it not knowing what's going to happen or what's being planned. You hear all these rumors in your company that someone starts. They may be true or they may not be true. You have no idea. There was talk of invading North Vietnam, or moving north, or going to An Lao Valley, and they were nothing more than rumors. You really don't know what's happening until you get there. Then, you look at what happened and that's the first time you really know. So, I tried not to take any of the rumors seriously, but they were hard to ignore. The uncertainty and confusion added to our stress. Being able to ignore the rumors and not be bothered by not knowing was a big part of staying sane.

I started my third month in late April and they were sending me back to An Khe for the leadership school I had missed before. I passed it this time. More importantly, being in An Khe gave me the chance to call Beth, Mom, and Dad by MARS. We could only talk for five minutes and I could not tell them my location. Dad wanted to know if I wanted a hunting knife. He had been in World War II, so he had a sense of what soldiers needed. I told him I would take a pocketknife. It was lighter and managing the weight I carried was important. I told them that I had started carrying more ammo, 700 rounds. It was more weight, but worth it to be sure I didn't run out when I needed it. I also told them that I was the acting squad leader until the regular squad leader got back from R&R. I said my captain had told me I would make a sergeant by August or September. I still hadn't gotten Spec 4, but that was supposed to happen this month.

Another good thing about being in An Khe was that I got to see a movie. I forget now which it was and didn't include that in the letter. One of the big films then was In Like Flint, the James Coburn spy comedy. It might have been that or One Million Years B.C., the caveman movie starring Raquel Welch. Whatever movie it was, it was a welcome escape from the war. And the heat.

On the bad side, An Khe was hit by a mortar attack that killed nine people. The base was mortared all the time, but it was big and the VC were always just hoping to hit anything. As I wrote in a letter, although nine might seem like a lot of people, it was not many on such a large base. It was like nine people dying in our town of Clovis, NM. The base at An Khe was about the same size.

Something else about Vietnam that we didn't have in the States was cobras. I saw a 4-foot one in the field and they killed and 11-foot one at An Khe. I sent a photo of it to Beth, Mom, and Dad. Between the Vietcong, panthers, and cobras it seemed like everything in this country was trying to kill us.

While we were still at the school, a forward observer – an officer who goes to the company to call in artillery fire – got shot in the eye. He would live, though, lucky for him. That's not usually something a person survives. It just goes to show how much survival is the luck of the draw. If that bullet had gone a fraction of an inch to the left, right, up, or down, he'd be dead. Instead, he gets to go back to his family alive. Yes, he's missing an eye and he'll probably be traumatized for a long time, but that beats being dead.

The whole base at An Khe is talking about moving north, invading North Vietnam. I told Beth and said not to say anything. It's supposed to be classified information. I don't know how a rumor can be classified. She won't tell anyone and there aren't any Communist spies in Clovis, so it's safe.

In a lot of my letters, it seems like I wrote about what I was into back then, rather than write much about the war. I wrote a lot about archery, which was my favorite pastime. I often enjoyed writing about that more than about what had happened in the war that day. I imagine Beth enjoyed hearing about archery more than about the war, too. I won't write much about it here, though, since archery isn't the subject of the book. Maybe that should be my next book. I'll write one every 50 years.

If you notice, I haven't said anybody's name in the letters (or this book). I don't know why, unless I just didn't know many of the other soldiers by name in this letter. I certainly don't remember more than a few of the names now. In the letter on May 8, I wrote about "my best friend," Rod Kowski. Honestly, I really don't remember him, but we were such good friends that I gave him Beth's address and he gave me his girlfriend's address, in case something happened to one of us. I say girlfriend, but he was actually engaged. Unfortunately, things turned badly for them while he was in Vietnam and she broke it off. He got really down in the dumps. This was a pretty common occurrence over there. Some wives and girlfriends couldn't handle being apart for so long. Or, maybe they couldn't handle the fear of something happening to their husband or boyfriend. It was easier and less painful to just end the relationship. Lots of guys took it pretty hard for a little while, but most of them bounced back. I don't remember now how much or how quickly Rod got over it.

As I was preparing this book, Beth went and looked up a bunch of names that were in the company. I appreciate her effort and will try to start mentioning the names as we go.

I graduated from the school on May 13 and stayed in An Khe a few more days. I'd earned it! I did really well in the school and finished in the top 10 out of 80. In the last couple days of the course, we made an air assault and then patrolled all day. I guess they thought we don't get enough of that out in the field. I'm not sure what the cadre in the rear thought they could teach us front line guys about air assaulting and patrolling. Anyway, I was happy to be there at the school, because I got to be in An Khe, rather than sleeping in a rice paddy. Upon graduating, I got a little piece of paper from the school. I spent the next day cleaning my weapon to turn it back in to the school and getting my junk in order. They want me to go back to the field the next day, but I talked the sergeant into letting me stay just one more day. We had a barbecue on that last night with steaks, beer, onion rings, and more beer – all free. I wrote to Beth about looking forward to taking R&R with her, even though it was a long way away.

I returned to the field on May 15 after 15 days. We had a nickname for people who were stationed in the rear. We call them "low quarters" after the shoes they wore. Instead of boots, they could wear low top dress shoes – low quarters – if they wanted to, because it was so safe and they didn't need the support or protection of boots, as they never went out in the bush on long patrols. We couldn't do that. We wouldn't make it two miles in those shoes. It was like there was a whole different army at places like An Khe. It's amazing the amount of support people it takes to make things work. You just almost have to be there to see what the rear echelon does to support the people out in the field. We may make fun of them and call them "low quarters" and worse, but we really did appreciate them. Without them, we wouldn't get paid, fed, promoted, rearmed, refueled, replaced, or medevacked. We wouldn't have any good intel about the enemy. No one would plan the war and give us our missions. We wouldn't get any mail, which was often the most important thing to me. So, I was okay with the "low quarters" and didn't mind spending 15 days with them.

I would now return to the company, leaving An Khe and the low quarters behind. As it turned out, though, we'd spend the next month operating in the vicinity of An Khe, which was okay by me.

# CHAPTER 7

FROM AN KHE back to my unit, I was first flown to LZ Uplift, which was about five miles from the ocean, and had to wait there for another chopper for a few hours. The company had made an air assault on the beach and captured 18 VC. That was a pretty big deal. And, I had missed it. I didn't mind.

The next day, while waiting for helicopters to come pick us up, we had to use explosives to blow up coconut trees, so the choppers could land. We blew up the trees to blow them down. Just a little joke. We took the coconuts and mixed Kool-Aid with the coconut juice and it made a good drink. If you leave soldiers by themselves for any time at all, they'll figure out some new ingenuity to make their lives better.

We were back at An Khe the next day, the whole company, and left the same day. We would be operating just outside of An Khe for 30 days. The first morning on patrol, we startled – and were startled by – a deer-like animal. It had horns and was really big. We were in pretty thick cover, but still managed to shoot at him. He escaped without injury. So did we. Another day, some guys started yelling that they saw a giant alligator. We grabbed our rifles and took off after him there. He was in this draw and everybody up opened up on him. Well, it wasn't an alligator, but a great big, five-foot iguana or maybe monitor lizard. It looked something like an alligator, but more like a prehistoric monster. It had serrated teeth and sharp claws. None of us felt badly at all about shooting it before it could eat us. The cobras, even the panthers, were probably preferred over this creature.

We went on an ambush one night, rested during the day while another squad went on patrol, then went on another ambush the next night. During this operation, I had started carrying the radio and there was a chance of doing it permanently. My sergeant had asked me about being the radio operator a while back. It is safer than walking point and crawling in caves, as I had been doing. Rereading the letters, it seems that I had been walking point for my platoon for a while. I don't remember when I started doing that or know for sure how long I did. It's more dangerous and stressful, not something most people want to do routinely or forever. Maybe I was good at it. I'll cover it in more detail a little later.

We were back to full strength. By that I mean about 130 men, not the authorized 150 to 160 or more. We'd never get to that, so in my mind, full strength was 130 or so. We were getting new recruits in, which helped a lot.

A chaplain came to the field and we had a church service. It was really nice. I'd like to write about that some more in a little while, if I can remember to do it. As I said before, I don't want to sound like a preacher, but religion did play a role in my Vietnam experience.

May 21, I was starting my fourth month in Vietnam. I wrote to Beth that nothing was going on and I hoped they'd fly out beer and soda for us. I think we paid, I don't know, $5 a month and they would fly out maybe once a week, maybe not that often, beer and soda pop iced down in garbage cans. We each got two or three cans, I forget exactly how many. You could have a mixture of beer and soda or all three beers or maybe they made us take one of each or something like that. It didn't really matter, because I could always trade my soda off to the younger ones for beer.

We switched with another squad, so that we did day patrols and they went out on night ambushes. That's a little different than we did later on in my tour. I guess we did it like this back at the start, staying on either day patrols or night ambush. As I described earlier, from about halfway through and toward the end of my tour, we either secured the perimeter, were on listening posts, or went on ambush, and you rotated every day. We were doing one of those three things every day from the middle through the end.

Two days after I wrote that I hoped they'd bring us beer, they did. As predicted, I got three beers. We went on patrol the next day.

After a few days in one spot, we moved 4,000 meters, or 2 1/2 miles, and set up camp again. I can't ever remember another period when we set up camp and stayed more than one day. It must have been because we were operating around An Khe that we could do this. I guess we could dig in and stay two or three days since it was fairly safe around there. Other than that, we moved every day and dug in at a different place every night. Another good thing that I wrote to Beth about was having a long range patrol ration for lunch again. It was great. It was the small pleasures that made me happy.

On May 25th, I got a big pleasure – a new ring to replace my lost wedding ring. Beth sent me her grandfather's wedding ring. It was a very nice thing for her to do and it made me feel very loved. In a way, losing my wedding ring ended up bringing me something very special, which wouldn't have happened if I hadn't lost the first ring. It was a silver lining that was quite touching, a terrific thing for her to do for me. I really, really enjoyed getting that ring from Beth. I also saw a lot of peacocks that day. Those beautiful birds in the middle of a combat zone on the day I got this new ring felt right.

A couple days later, I got another package from home. It couldn't top the new wedding ring, but it was still pretty good – a thick envelope with archery magazines and other archery info. I was big into archery back home, practiced it often, hunted with a bow, and even competed sometimes. You might wonder what archery news could fill a magazine every month. Well, there were new products, competition results, hunting photos of game that was shot, profiles of the best archers, tips on shooting techniques and equipment care, and the like. It was also another way to stay connected to the world outside of the war, to know that America went on as usual while we were away, that I'd have all that to go back to at the end of my tour. It also gave me something to write about with Beth, Mom, and Dad, besides the war. A couple of the other guys liked looking through the magazines, even though they weren't involved in the sport. Maybe they'd take it up when they got home. Some of the ads had pretty women, so that might have been the main thing they were interested in. I didn't ask.

The easy duty continued with more day patrols, although there was talk about going North or to the Cambodian border. It was just talk and rumors, as always, and I ignored most of it. Some of it could come true, but I'd deal with that if and when it happened.

Around this time, Mom wrote about Dad being possessive. I guess Mother thought he was telling Beth what to do and trying to get her to go to these archery tournaments with him and stuff like that. There wasn't much I could do about it from 14,000 miles away. I told her that Beth could stand up for herself, if she felt it was a problem. She was tough enough. I didn't really need drama from home distracting me. I guess I shouldn't complain. Other guys had much worse drama and it sometimes affected them in the field. At least, my wife still loved me and was awaiting my return.

We got to go to An Khe to clean up, which is always a physical and emotional relief. By 5:00, we were back in the boonies. We came back the next morning to get paid, another welcome event, and then were trucked out to highway 19 to protect it for two weeks. By protect it, I mean we made sure it was safe for friendly traffic. We generally stayed in one place, but sometimes patrolled the length of the highway in our assigned area, checking for VC or any bobby traps. Again, I heard that we are supposed to go to Cambodian border after these two weeks. For now, I'm taking advantage of this operation and trying to rest up. One nice part of this tasking was that we lived in bunkers while guarding the highway, with a roof over our heads. It's where we spent most of our time. It wasn't the Ritz, but it was better than what we normally had to sleep under, two ponchos tied together.

Looking back, it's clear that we were in a safe area and easy duty, because I was writing to Beth almost every day. On May 31, I wrote to her that the sergeant is talking about making me a squad leader in about two weeks. I still hadn't been promoted to Spec 4 and a PFC couldn't lead a squad that included Spec 4s. So, I guess the sergeant thought I'd get Spec 4 in about two weeks. We'll see.

We had been assigned to guard an artillery battery on highway 19. One night, we had some excitement. We captured six gooks. It all started when, during the day, we received some sniper fire. No one was hit and we never did get the snipers, but that same day at about dusk, a truck stopped in the vicinity of where the sniper fire had come from and picked up two gooks who had run out of the woods. The patrol that spotted them radioed to us as to what they saw and we were ordered to stop the truck, which we did. By this time, it was dark. After getting the five occupants out of the truck, I was told to search the back end. As I crawled over the tailgate, I was surprised to see one of these gooks looking at me right in the face from his hiding spot. I jumped back on the ground and pulled out my .45 pistol and went back in for him a second later. I ordered him to get out, but he was either too scared or didn't understand me, because he didn't move. No problem. I proceeded to evacuate him and he went out headfirst, with my help. We searched the six of them and the truck, then turned them over to the MPs, who interrogated them and confirmed that they were VC.

Other than that, it was pretty peaceful. We hadn't had a church service in a while and I missed having one.

June 4, it rained day and night with a lot of thunder – except the thunder was 105 Howitzers going off about 20 yards from us. As you can imagine, that made it hard to sleep. On the plus side, the army had taught me to sleep through anything. It might not have been a deep or continuous sleep, but it was better than nothing. Even without the artillery, when not on base, we didn't sleep too deeply, because we were always alert for the sound of something that wasn't right, something that could kill us. This included when it wasn't our turn to be on watch, because there was always the small possibility that the guy on watch had fallen asleep himself, so our ears were always partially awake. As we slept, we heard the pitter-patter of rats running around us and on the roof. We had no traps to catch them, so we had to put up with them.

I can remember one artillery post that we were securing somewhere during the tour, a different time than this. I had tied my poncho to the side of this motorized cannon. That's what it was, just a big cannon on tracks, like a bulldozer's caterpillar tread. At about 2:00 in the morning, that thing shot and dust came up and scared me to death. I never did tie my poncho up to another gun like that again.

We weren't doing much, just sitting in the bunkers, passing time by playing cards. It was really raining in the first week, a big gully washer. We spent most of the night fixing the bunker, so it wouldn't leak (much). That's one nice thing about the artillery places where we secured. They always had bunkers around them for us to stay in.

Today was a good example of how our army operates. We had an inspection. That's right, the colonel came out in the field and inspected us. He looked over our uniforms, haircuts, and weapons. I don't know if I passed or not and couldn't care less. I wanted to ask if there wasn't something more important, he could be doing or how us passing inspection would help us win the war or go home sooner. It was ridiculous. He probably got a medal for it. We went back to playing cards almost before he left.

We moved from the artillery group to a bridge we would guard. As the gooks went by on their motor scooters, we threw rocks in the air and watched them scramble to avoid them. We had to do something to pass the time.

Another day, we killed some time by chasing cows. We got some cornered and one of them fell into a big hole. We jumped on her and took turns riding her. It may not be the kind of thing you'd see on the news or in a war movie, but it was a lot of fun for us.

This fun was interrupted when the captain came around with a sheet of paper and asked everyone where they wanted to go on R&R. That's "rest and relaxation" or "rest and recuperation," another army term for vacation or leave. I guess when you're in a combat zone, leave is called R&R. I put in for Hawaii, which Beth and I had discussed and agreed on, and he said that I would more than likely get it. For R&R, Hawaii was usually set aside for the officers to bring their wives over. Most of the enlisted men were single and they went to Bangkok, Australia, and places like that. I told him I'd wait for Hawaii, knowing that it would be longer for me to get it, but I didn't mind waiting to have the chance to see Beth and give her a little Hawaiian vacation. She deserved it.

We moved to another bridge to secure it. It is the same old thing, but more gooks to watch. It rained all day and night and there was no sign of it letting up. I already liked the other bridge better (even if it was surely raining just as much there). We spent a lot of the time holed up under the bridge.

There was a pineapple field next to the bridge. Five of us went down to pick some out. A young girl came out of the house and told us she would pick some for us. After she did, she told us to follow her to the house. We went inside where her dad was waiting. She took the pineapples and skillfully cut the eyes out and cut them into slices and quarters. The Papasan (the dad) got shot glasses out and put them on the table. He then got a bottle that contained clear liquid and poured everyone a shot. We just stood there and looked at him. Finally, he picked one up and drank it, yelled "hi-yah," and went into a karate stance. Then, he took the cut up pineapple and ate it. We watched him and he didn't die, so we thought we would try it. After drinking a gulp, we understood why he yelled. It was strong as hell and tasted nasty.

He sold us the bottle, which was rice whiskey, and gave us the pineapples and we went back to the bridge. (The way I remembered it, we just took the whiskey, but in my letter to Beth, I wrote that we paid him for it.) We stood in a circle and passed the bottle around. After a while, when it was turn for the guy next to me to take a drink, he pulled out his .45 pistol and gave it to me. He told me to hold it to his head, which I did. He then took a drink and told me that was the only way he could get it down. It was a little drastic, but I understood. The squad leader got drunk and didn't want to get up to pull his shift guard duty. Me and another guy pulled him out and threatened to whip him if he didn't. He decided to pull his guard. I couldn't go to sleep, because I was afraid he would fall asleep on duty. I got up about 15 minutes later and sure enough, he was asleep. I went and woke up the other guy and together we carried the squad leader down to the river and threw him in. After that, he stayed awake and we were able to get some sleep.

The next night, our sleep was interrupted again in an unusual way. At about 3:45 in the morning, there was a loud animal scream. Everyone jumped up awake and saw some kind of wild cat about the size of a big bobcat. He had come down to the river for a drink, then caught our scent and crept over to investigate. He might have thought we might be tasty or, more likely, have food lying around for him to steal. Our sudden movement spooked him though, because in the second it took us to grab our guns, he was gone. It spooked us, too, and we kind of laughed it off nervously.

Guess what the gooks were selling us next. Popsicles. I don't know how they made them or who they learned it was a treat we had back home, but they did. They had a piece of bamboo in them for a stick and, surprisingly, they were good. Anytime you were around bridges or artillery bases, there were Vietnamese children selling beer, soda pop, gum, everything else. Anything to make some money. They were very entrepreneurial in that way, very business-minded. If Vietnam hadn't later become a Communist country and that natural capitalist tendency had been allowed to thrive, some of those kids might have become successful business owners. Maybe some of the ones that went to America did succeed. I don't know. In the small New Mexico town where Beth and I ended up living after the war, the only Vietnamese I ever saw were in a few Vietnamese restaurants. So, I suppose those did become business owners, some successful.

That day, we walked over to a big building and went in and, to my surprise, it was a real nice pig house with concrete pens. And, they had American pigs in it. The US built it for these people and gave them the pigs. We played with the baby pigs for a little while. The workers at the place didn't care, but they might have wondered why we would have fun playing with baby pigs that were just for food.

Some Montagnard people lived around here and they were the closest thing to savages that I have ever seen. I don't mean they were mean or threatening. In fact, they were quiet and kept to themselves. We didn't interact much with them and they basically ignored us, although both sides stared at each other out of curiosity. They had beautiful crossbows and are really primitive. The men wore only a loincloth and the women were bare from the waist up, with only a blanket around the lower half of their bodies. They smoked marijuana in a crude, simple pipe. They took some kind of black junk from a tree and put it on their teeth and turn them black, which is supposed to be a sign of beauty, at least that's what I understood. It didn't look beautiful to me, but beauty is in the eye of the beholder. The Vietnamese people hated the Montagnards and vice versa, although I think they fought against the North Vietnamese, mostly alongside the American Green Berets.

I received an envelope from home with a St. Christopher medal, which I really did appreciate. I still wear it to this day, half a century later. The priest that married us gave Beth the medal to send to me, Father Joe Fasel of Saint James Episcopal Church in Clovis. He had been in the Coast Guard in World War II and Korea. My faith was important to me. My mother was the daughter of a minister, so maybe that's what instilled religion in me. I didn't wear the medal for St. Cristopher's protection, nor did I pray to be kept safe. I knew lots of men who wore crosses and still got shot. I just wore it to remind me of my beliefs.

I saw a truck run over a little boy. From the looks of him, he would probably die. He ran right in front of the truck that was going about 35 miles an hour. I could see that it tore him up pretty good. I only mentioned this in passing in my letters. It wasn't a moment that stands out in my memory. I saw a lot of people die in Vietnam. This was just another one. There were a lot of kids everywhere, not just selling us things. Sometimes, kids would even sleep under the bridges with us. I don't know if they didn't have homes to go to or what. Maybe they slept under bridges all the time and we just happened to be there, too.

I had forgotten Mother's Day and Father's Day, but wrote to my mother and father to wish them a belated happy Mother's Day and Father's Day. I mailed the letter a little before Father's Day, but there was no way it would get there in time. I imagine they understood that I had a few other things on my mind.

On June 13, we went to An Khe for about three or four days. I wrote to Beth that I hoped to be in a position to call her for our anniversary on June 16. I also wrote that one of the other guys had requested to go to sniper school and wrote more about archery. Some of the things I wrote may seem now like a mix of random topics, but they were things going on in my life over there and things that I thought about.

We learned that the reason we were back at An Khe wasn't for a stand down (a short time to relax), but to act as the reactionary force. This meant we were on a 15-minute alert, in case the base was attacked or we had to support another unit that was under attack in the field. I talked to the sergeant and told him I wanted to call home on the 15th for our anniversary. We were supposed to leave on the 17th and we were only allowed to make phone calls on odd number days, I don't know why. He said it was okay, so I hoped I would get to call Beth as an anniversary present for her.

It turned out that I was able to call her on June 15, the day before our anniversary. The MARS connection was horrible and we weren't able to communicate well at all. I was still happy to be able to wish her a happy one-year anniversary and tell her I loved her. I heard her say the same to me, which really made me feel great. I hope she was able to hear me well enough, because those were important words.

I forgot to tell Beth either in the call or in a letter that I finally got my promotion to Spec 4. I did tell my parents in a letter to them. The promotion came two and a half months after I was put in for it. The army can work fast when it needs to, but generally takes forever to get anything done. The two and a half months of extra pay would have come in handy for Beth back home. Oh well, we were grateful for it now.

I sent Beth my Silver Star medal for safe keeping. I also sent her my watch that had gotten broken and asked her to get it fixed. This was in a letter I wrote on June 16, our anniversary. I wrote to her about that and how it made me happy to hear her voice on that day.

Our time of easier duty was finally coming to an end and talking to Beth on our anniversary was a fitting way to finish that short safer time. It had been nice, but there was still a war going on and we had to get back to the thick of it.

# CHAPTER 8

BY JUNE 20, we were back in the field for at least three more months. This was about three months after our big battle, so we had gotten a fair amount of time to get replacements for the men we had lost and to get our heads back into the right shape. Just as important, it was three months closer to finishing my tour and going home. I was now close to the end of my fourth month in Vietnam and I found myself in the biggest and hardest battle since the big battle in the graveyard on March 20.

We went to LZ Uplift to secure it for three days. There were rumors that McNamara would drop in to see the base. I would have liked to give him a piece of my mind, although I doubted he would be asking for our opinions on how he was running the war. As Secretary of Defense for Presidents Kennedy and Johnson, he was largely responsible for the buildup of troops in Vietnam and, therefore, for me being there. Although he had served in World War II, his background was in business and his service was mostly in the Army Air Forces' Office of Statistical Control. So, he was all about numbers and body counts. He really didn't understand if we were winning or losing on the ground.

I had been made a fire team leader. A fire team is half a squad, which put me over four men, including a machine gunner, assuming we had everyone. The new recruits brought us up to close to "full strength." There are a lot of new faces. It was good to have the manpower, but having so many troops with no combat experience was a little troubling. I guess we were all green once and it doesn't take much to figure out what to do when someone shoots at you. As fire team leader, I would be one of the people responsible for helping the new guys learn quickly, so they could stay alive and do us some good.

B Company got hit pretty hard and one platoon was down to only 10 men, which means they lost half to two-thirds of the platoon's men. I heard that the company lost 100, but that was probably an exaggeration or just bad info. Or, maybe it was the company, not the platoon, that was down to 10 men, which would be a terrible amount of casualties, dead and wounded. Whatever the exact numbers, B Company had taken a beating and we needed to help them out. We didn't know how many VC they were fighting, but we knew it was a lot. It had to be to cause so many losses.

Once B Company had a sense of the force they were up against and how badly they were outnumbered, we were immediately called to air assaulted in. The whole area was infested with Vietcong. Already today, they had had 23 air strikes in this one area, which is a lot. We no sooner landed when we made contact. It wasn't as bad as the battle on March 20, but it was bad enough.

We were fighting up in the mountains and it was really thick jungle. I was walking point, which means I was the lead guy, typically the first person to make contact. At one point, I stopped for a minute to take a breather. We were already all exhausted. As I caught my breath, I looked just in front of me and saw what it looked like a pair of black pants lying on the ground. I kept looking and then spotted two feet sticking out of the pants. It was a dead VC. We had to search him and, of course, you-know-who was elected to do that. I didn't find anything of value on him, such as maps or any intel, so we just left him and continued on.

I really don't remember when I started walking point, but from the letters, it seems that I had already been doing it for a while now. I don't know if I was broken into it with training from someone else or just started being the point man, on the job training. Each platoon had someone designated to walk point, which means that every time my platoon led the company, I was on point. We rotated platoons, so I was the lead guy for the company every third day. Later, on another mission, I walked point three straight days and told the company first sergeant they had better get someone else tomorrow, because I had had enough. He said he would. I was good at what I did, which was one reason I didn't mind doing it so often. The guy behind me was Coble and Sandusky was behind him. Coble took everything to the right, watching for any enemy in that direction. Sandusky took everything to the left. I took everything in front. The front was usually where we would run into the enemy.

The heat was unreal. We were in the mountains with real thick jungle, which we had to chop through with our machetes. Since I was on point, that meant I had to do most of the chopping. It was miserable and grueling. Our platoon had three men pass out from heat exhaustion. Another platoon had seven pass out. It was so bad that we had to be resupplied by chopper twice with more water. I had taken six salt tablets to help my body retain water and I was still dizzy and weak. Our legs and bodies cramped up, too. It was not an optimal condition to fight a battle. As we started back up, everybody was really in bad shape. It was plain to see we couldn't make it, so they air lifted us back out, which sure saved the day.

They moved us down in the valley where we were searching everything for more VC. The whole valley was covered with a haze of smoke and the VC were still fighting. Things were pretty hairy around there. Everywhere we went, we ran into the enemy. We even ran into a bunch of VC reinforcements and had it out with them. I had never seen such a big force pour in one area.

We had come off this mountain and halfway down into the valley, we ran into a VC regimental headquarters. Most of the regiment had taken off and left just enough fighters behind to hold us back, while the rest got out of there. They left everything behind except their weapons and ammo. When we finally moved in, we found bunkers, packs, food, medical supplies, spare barrels for the machine guns, and a bunch of other stuff. They were really set up with bunkers all over the place. They had a complete hospital set up. I don't know why they didn't stay and fight us, as they could really have messed us up. There were well over 200 bunkers with two men to a bunker, so you can see how many there were. We called in an airstrike and they pretty well worked over the area, destroying the bunkers and anyone who may have stuck around. By then, the VC were gone or on the run, so they air lifted us out to LZ English. When we left, there were over 100 dead VC by body count. You don't know how lucky we were, because those VC were set up in an excellent place for an ambush and they could have wiped us out.

A couple days before, our platoon had gone down that way and shot a VC. He was wounded really bad and we followed his blood trail. It was really hot, so our lieutenant told us to take a break. I actually fell asleep in the middle of the trail. When I woke up, I was covered in mud from my sweat mixing with the dirt in the trail. We didn't bring any chow – C rations – with us. The lieutenant used this as an excuse (my opinion) to go back and join the company, so we turned back. We were lucky we did, because just our platoon would have followed that blood trail right into that regimental headquarters and we would have been in for a big surprise. The next day we went back with the full company and the Vietcong were gone.

Back at LZ English, Beth and I were planning by letter to take R&R in the middle of August. Two single guys that came over at the same time as me would be having their R&Rs starting July 15. Because I had asked for Hawaii, where most officers went and got first choice, which meant the rest of us, the enlisted men, had to wait. That's why Beth and I would get our R&R in August. That would be about halfway through my tour in Vietnam, so it seemed right, anyway. It was about a month and a half away and I was counting the days.

On July 1, I wrote that the other day the 2nd of the 5th Calvary, a sister battalion of ours, got hit and they air assaulted us in from LZ English to help them. We had the VC surrounded in a village by the sea. We were airlifted in from the seaward side, which was pretty cool, coming in low over the waves. We had big sand dunes to hide behind. They mostly hid our helicopter insertion as well as giving us cover and concealment for our firing positions. We called in air strikes and artillery to "soften up" the target. The gunship helicopters came in and strafed the village, several runs of that. Some of the enemy tried to escape that attack by running out toward the sea, but quickly discovered we were waiting there to shoot them. Those that didn't get shot ran back into the village. Any that tried to escape on the inland side found 2nd Battalion waiting for them. Then, here came the helicopters again and it would start all over. It was a lot of fun for us, not so much for the VC. It was a big village, so this battle went on for a long time. The VC kept shooting, so we kept up the attack. It went on through the night.

The next day, we went down to the village and got online to sweep it. They brought five tanks in and I was lined up right beside one. It was the first time I had been so close to a tank in battle. I had seen them in training, but never in action. They were so heavy and powerful that the ground shook when they moved. That's no exaggeration. We got the order to move out and, without warning, that tank fired its big gun. I hit the ground so fast my helmet came down and cut my nose. I yelled at the tank commander, calling him a few choice words. It didn't matter, because he couldn't hear me over the rumble of the tank.

As we started through the village, if it moved, we shot it. This included pigs, dogs, chickens, and other livestock, not that we wanted to shoot animals. We were just trying to stay alive and deal with an enemy in hiding. We shot a water buffalo, which was a big mistake, because they don't die easily. We finally had to finish it off with a machine gun. One VC ran into a small house. We opened the door and the whole room was filled with big vases, about waist tall. We figured he was in one of those. We didn't know which one, So, we just threw a few grenades in there and shut the door.

We came to a well and were in the process of filling our canteens with good, cold water, which we desperately needed by then. A sergeant walked up and threw a hand grenade down the well and said it wasn't fit to drink. It sure wasn't after that! I have no idea why he didn't want us taking that water, but we didn't care for him much from then on.

Because we were in the role of reactionary force, we didn't stay in the village once the battle was over. Instead, we were flown back to LZ English to wait for the next time we would be needed. When another company got hit, we would go in and help them. It could be a busy job or a slow one, depending on what was happening with the other companies. We spent a lot of time sitting and waiting. It beat hiking around in the heat and it was better to be the responders than the ones who were in need of help.

Our company commander rotated to the rear on June 30 and we are waiting for a new one. I hope he isn't as gung ho as the last one. Gung ho officers usually translates to crap for the soldiers, either greater risk or less comfort. I don't know if the officers are trying to prove how heroic they are or that they're such great leaders, but neither is true. It's the soldiers that bear the brunt of them being gung ho. Medals for officers often means the enlisted men have either suffered more or died. There's nothing heroic about that. Anyway, back to what I was saying. Officers only have to stay in the field six months. Then, they are rotated back to the rear for the remainder of their tour. This is another one of those things that I don't know the reason for. Maybe it's so more officers can have combat leadership positions. If each person's time in the field is half as long, then you need twice as many people. Or, maybe they need more officers doing work in the rear, whatever work that might be. As I mentioned, the "low quarters" do a lot of work that's needed to keep everything in the field running well. Whatever the reason, the officers spend half the time in harm's way than enlisted men do. So, you can see why we resented when the commanders reduced the time before the end of our tour that we rotated to the rear. They rotated with six months to go, but reduced our one month to 15 days and then 7 days. Not cool.

On July 1, LZ Crystal got mortared during the night. It was about 20 miles south of LZ English. We were put on 15-minute alert, but were never called out. I'm really looking forward to R&R, or as soldiers called is I&I for Intercourse and Intoxication. I wrote this in a letter to Beth, but not to my parents. On July 4, LZ English got heavily mortared and it got pretty hot for a while. It wasn't on our part of the base, though, and our platoon wasn't in any real danger. Our new company commander still hadn't arrived. We spend the days sitting around and waiting. At LZ English, we got three hot meals a day and showers, so we were happy to stay there and not go on any missions. July 5, still no new commander. On July 6, I told Beth I was writing the letter in a bunker and a snake crawled in. I couldn't find where it went. Finally, I just gave up and went back to writing. If it was still in there, I would find out eventually, one way or another. It probably just slithered out while I was looking for it. There were a lot more dangerous things to worry about in Vietnam.

On July 8, I wrote about a short guy from Lubbock, Texas by the name of Freddy Ramirez. He was a funny guy, good-natured with a good sense of humor. I remember he took a lot of razzing for being Mexican and for his accent. We teased him really badly. He took it in good spirits and was always laughing. He was a good guy and we laughed all the time. Still no new commander, but he's supposedly arriving tomorrow.

On July 9, I only had time to write a short note to Beth, because they told us we were moving out and had to pack up.

On July 13, the new commander finally arrived and he was a real SOB. We had gone two weeks without a commander and done just fine. Now, the best they could find for us was this jerk. He had just gotten word that he was to be promoted to major – company commander is a position for a captain, and major was one rank higher – so we'd be getting rid of him soon. Not soon enough for my liking. The first night, he woke us up at midnight and had us walk the rest of the night and all the next day. It was raining a lot and we had to sleep wet. None of us had any idea what the objective of the patrol was, maybe movement to contact. Whatever the reason, our first days with this new commander were miserable and pointless, which was a sign of what was to come. At one point during the day, the VC sneaked up and threw grenades at us, wounding one person. I had to walk point and we were chasing some 125 VC. "Chasing" is a little bit of an exaggeration, because I made sure we never caught them. It would have been stupid to chase a battle where we were outnumbered like that. So, I worked my way through the brush carefully and slowly. Somehow, they got away.

On July 15, I wrote to Beth from LZ Ollie about six miles south of Bong Son. I had been told I would make sergeant soon. This was only a month after being promoted to specialist 4, which I waited about two and a half months for after being told I would get it. I learned this time not to get too excited, because who knew when it would actually happen.

Military ranks are often referred to by their equivalent pay grade, which is a letter and a number. The three private ranks correspond to the pay grades E-1, E-2, and E3. Specialist is E-4 and so is corporal. In our unit at the time I was in Vietnam, E-4s were all called specialist 4, not corporal. I think the army changed its practice of using the term corporal over the years. It didn't matter to me, as long as the pay was the same. The ranks above that were all variations of sergeant. E-5 was just called sergeant. E-6 was staff sergeant and, in the infantry, was usually a squad leader, although some E-6s were platoon sergeants and some E-5s were squad leaders, because we were so understaffed. Platoon sergeants were supposed to be E-7, sergeant first class, but we only had a couple of those in the entire company. We did have the one allotted E-8, first sergeant. The only remaining enlisted rank was E-9, which was the sergeant major of the battalion and all organizational levels above battalion. In the officer ranks, as the organizational levels went higher, the rank and pay grade of the person in charge went up, too. A battalion commander was a lieutenant colonel (O-5), brigade commander was a colonel (O-6), division commander was a two-star general or major general (O-8), and so on up to four-star general (O-10). Brigadier generals (one-stars) aren't usually commanders of units, which seems a little weird to me. You finally make general and don't get to be in command of anything. Oh well. The other thing that seems weird is that the top enlisted soldiers in each unit, the command sergeant major, doesn't advance in pay grade. A battalion sergeant major, who oversees the non-commissioned officer supervisory chain for about 800 soldiers, is the same rank as the top enlisted soldier in the army. For officers, the very top person is four ranks higher than a battalion commander. I didn't give it too much thought, though. That sort of thing was literally above my pay grade.

Instead of focusing on a possible promotion, I wrote to Beth about how much I was looking forward to our upcoming R&R. That was much more on my mind than if I would ever get promoted again and when.

A couple days later, I received a box from women in Slaton, Texas where, Pat, my sister, was teaching. Slaton is just outside of

Lubbock and about 120 miles southeast of Clovis. Pat must have told them about me serving in Vietnam and they decided to show their support of us with a care package. In the package, were five boxes of Tide detergent. Everybody cracked up. It was nice of the women and we were thankful that they cared about us, but we didn't have any washing machines in the field, so no way to use the Tide. We sold it to the Vietnamese for three dollars. Tide probably cost about 50 cents a carton back then, so we came out ahead (not counting the postage and packaging).

Between looking forward to seeing Beth, receiving a thoughtful and amusing care package, and maybe someday getting promoted again, it was a welcome brief interlude in the madness of war. More was to surely to come.

# CHAPTER 9

IN COMBAT, THE higher ups would sometimes dictate what were called rules of engagement. The point of these were basically to keep noncombatants from getting killed by accident. The idea was to only shoot at people that we knew were enemy.

We had come back from an ambush patrol and were about to go on another, when the new captain called us together and said we had 10 rules of engagement. He had not come up with these rules, but rather they were dictated to us from the higher ups in the rear who didn't know their heads from a hole in the ground about combat engagement. They included: return fire when fired upon, fire when told by higher command, yell "dong lee" and fire a warning shot, and more than I can remember. Once he finished his little speech, he asked if there were any questions and nobody said anything.

Although I didn't immediately speak up, I had a big problem with these rules from on high, people who had nothing better to do than send down stupid orders that they didn't have to follow and bear the consequences of – potentially deadly consequences.

The captain commanded, "Okay, let's move out. Hoy, you have point."

I answered, "No, sir."

He said, "What?" with a look of total incomprehension.

I explained, "You can walk point and wait for somebody to shoot at you first, before you could shoot back." This was not the usual way a specialist spoke to a major and he was caught off guard.

He looked at me for some time. I didn't know if he would try to order me to take point, charge me with insubordination, or what. Instead, he came back with, "Disregard those orders. We'll find a hand grenade or something by the person if we shot them."

I nodded and said, "Yes, sir" and we moved out.

The major was smart enough to listen to a junior soldier who had spent much more time in combat than he had, which sort of impressed me, especially since he had probably put a lot of thought and time into writing those rules of engagement.

You have to understand, where we are operating was not in a town with lots of people, but out in the jungle where nobody except the enemy is supposed to be. So, we'd shoot anything that moved to keep us from getting killed, which was kind of important to us. The difference between dying and surviving was usually a split second, not enough time for a warning shot, much less shouting "dong lee," whatever that meant. Yes, there were times we'd go down to a village. Sometimes the villages were pretty big, but it was just women and children. And no, we didn't shoot anybody that moved there. We had common sense and it was based on months of combat experience. Lots of our buddies had left as casualties, but we were still there in one piece and had learned from each firefight we had survived. We also learned from each woman or child that we didn't mistakenly shoot. When you're out in the jungle, out in the boonies where nobody's supposed to be, and you're on point and somebody jumps out in front of you, you have no choice, but to shoot him. And, that's almost always the right choice, the choice that leaves a VC dead or wounded and you and your squad one day closer to going home to our loved ones. Dong lee, my ass.

Sometimes, our experience fails us, like when a terrible thing happened on July 18. One of the men in my platoon killed his buddy. He was cleaning his weapon, which he thought was empty, when he accidentally fired it and the bullet hit his buddy, who was sitting across from him, in the chest. The medic tried to save him and did a real good job. The medic hit him in the chest to get his heart beating and gave him mouth to mouth resuscitation to get him breathing again. Despite these efforts, the soldier died just before they got him to the hospital. The guy who shot him was in really bad shape. He had been cleaning his weapon and thought it was clear. He had the magazine out, but didn't realize there was still a round in the chamber. This happens in rare instances, due to lack of sleep, weariness, and exhaustion. After removing the magazine, the soldier is supposed to pull the charging handle back to eject any round that might still be in the chamber. The next step is to pull the trigger. He apparently neglected the middle step. When he pulled the trigger, his weapon was pointed the wrong way and he shot his friend.

The guy was sent to the rear for a week to regain his sanity and deal with bureaucratic stuff related to the accident. He was fined $50 and charged with involuntary manslaughter. The army had to do that, so the dead guy's parents couldn't file additional charges and make a long, drawn out deal over it – not that they would, but it was for the soldier's protection.

When he was sent back to the field, he refused to carry a weapon. You know, it was a tragic deal and the guy was pretty shook up. So, when he came back to the field, he said, "No, I'm not carrying a weapon." I don't know if he was afraid of hurting another friend or if he might have thought he deserved to get killed himself. Everyone is affected by something like that differently and responds in their own way. This was his way, although only for a short time. It didn't take long before we were in a firefight and he was caught out there being shot at. Whatever his reason had been for not carrying a weapon disappeared as soon as the bullets started flying and he realized he wanted to live or needed to do his part in battle. So, he grabbed a weapon and started shooting and carried one from then on.

A couple days later, we patrolled by a stream and got to bathe – always a treat. A day or two later, our mission took us to the beach and we were able to go swimming, which was great. In case you're wondering, just like when we're at a stream, at the beach we take turns, with some guys swimming and the rest providing security, in case the VC have plans for a day at the beach.

Another treat was that my buddy, Ron Coble, the guy who walked behind me when I was on point, had just gotten back from R&R in Malaysia and brought back a fifth of Seagram's 7, which he was kind enough to share with me. It was really good. When soldiers talked about R&R, we would always joke that all the guys came back with the clap and broke. Well, Coble came back with a fifth of Seagram's 7, which is a much better way to come back. He might have also had the clap and been broke, but that wasn't my concern. In fact, at that moment, it wasn't Coble's concern either.

On July 22, the company got up at 3:00 in the morning and walked all day. We first swept a village, checking for any VC, weapons, maps, or other intel or evidence that the VC operated from the village. Although we didn't find anything to confirm that it was a VC village, what happened later suggested that the VC had, at the very least, been alerted to our presence. After the sweep, we moved to a little hill nearby that overlooked the surrounding area. That night, in the bright moonlight, we spotted sixteen VC crossing a rice paddy. Second Platoon went after them and its platoon sergeant hit a booby trap. The blast hurt him and three members of the platoon. It's possible that the VC had purposely exposed themselves to draw American soldiers to where the booby trap was.

To avoid running into any further traps or ambushes, air support was called in, rather than the platoon continuing the pursuit on foot. This was the first time I witnessed a B-52 strike. It was impressive. A B-52 carried 108 500-pound bombs or a mix of 500-pound and 750-pound bombs that were used for "carpet bombing." Our artillery support, in comparison, fired 100-pound rounds, up to four per minute. The B-52 attack did a lot more damage and did it faster. We got down in our foxholes when we knew the strike was about to happen, but couldn't resist peeking to get a look. The entire area where the VC had been and the area where we planned to go the next day went up in a long series of large explosions. We could feel the heat in the rush of air that washed over us. We searched the area the next day and found that the bombing had really done some damage. It was amazing to see the destruction. The craters were as big as parking lots. Nothing could've survived that attack. It was unreal.

The next night, my fire team had to go on ambush patrol. We just got set up in a position along a trail, when we heard on the radio that another team that had set up in a different position not far away, got surrounded by VC and had to fight their way out of there. Needless to say, we didn't get any sleep that night. When you're on ambush, you go out with anywhere from six to eight guys. One guy will be on watch and the others are able to get some sleep. And then you rotate probably about every two hours. The guy on watch alerts the others when he spots enemy approaching, or the other soldiers will hear them coming, or the VC will set off the trip flare. In any case, there's no need for everyone to stay awake. But this night, knowing the VC were in the area looking for us – and probably pissed off about their losses in the carpet bombing – none of us got any sleep.

Back at LZ Uplift, I receive the bad news that orders for R&R came down for August and I wasn't on it. It will probably be in September. Once again, the officer's got priority over the enlisted man. Needless to say, this was a big disappointment for Beth and me. This was the one thing we had both been looking forward to for months. We had gotten our hopes up for August and, although we understood that it might get bumped, we allowed ourselves to expect good news. So, this was a real blow to our spirits. We tried to console each other and readjust our expectations and accept that one more month wasn't so bad – even if it felt like it was. Damn army.

In other bad news, I heard from a guy at An Khe, where all our personal gear was stored, that someone had broken into my duffel bag and stolen my tape recorder, which had been lent to me by my sister-in-law and her husband, Sue and Artie. So, I wouldn't be able to listen to any tapes that Beth might send me or record anything for her. We were already only writing letters and not sending tapes, but now we couldn't if we wanted to. Plus, it upset me that I couldn't return what Sue and Artie were nice enough to send me. On top of that, I lent my movie camera to another soldier who went on R&R a couple of months ago and he lost it. He has yet to pay for it, despite me hounding him for the money. I finally decided to go to the first sergeant, the top NCO in the company, and tell him the story. He said that he will make sure that I get my money this payday. With all that goes on in war, little things like this are big irritations. You'd think soldiers would take care of each other to get through it all as smoothly as possible. Not everyone thinks that way, apparently. I guess people who are jerks back in the world are still jerks in war.

The last week or so of July consisted of a lot of hiking up and down mountains, based out of LZ Uplift. We were constantly getting up at 3:00 and climbing mountains all day long. One day, I had point and we ended up having a dog handler and a dog with us. Boy, I sure did like working with one, as he was exceptionally smart – the dog, that is. (The handler was also pretty good.) This dog was a German shepherd and really knew what he was doing. His handler would tell him to search and he would take off in front of me, sniffing and looking all around. He would detect the booby traps before any of us would and just sit down and not move. This was his signal to us that he had found a booby trap. We went up this one mountain in thick jungle and came upon a small clearing where a bomb had cleared away the brush. The dog stopped dead in his tracks and started barking. We hit the ground and threw grenades to the opposite side of the clearing. Sure enough, there was a VC sniper waiting for us. The grenades wounded him and we finished him off. That dog saved our skins. He was one of the smartest dogs I ever saw in my entire life.

A couple days later, after walking all day long, we set up for the night in an abandoned rice paddy. There was nothing comfortable about that location and it kind of left us out in the open. At least we could see anyone approaching us from a long way off. It was impossible for the VC to sneak up on us. About this time, I got a letter from my parents saying that Bud, my Dad, had bought a pool hall in Clovis and was all excited about it. It was kind of weird to be sitting in an abandoned rice paddy thinking about my Dad buying a pool hall. That seemed like an entire world away. I was happy for him, although it was hard to get excited about it from my perspective.

In my first letter to Beth in August, I wrote that we climbed a mountain during the daytime and went down it at night to circle a village. I didn't write anything else about it, so I guess nothing came from that. It was probably a suspected VC location, but we didn't see anything to confirm that.

The next day, I was chosen to go to an artillery class that was to be held right where we were in the boonies. I guess the higher ups had decided we needed more people who knew how to call for fire support and it had to happen right now. Typical army. Part of the class would be me actually calling in an artillery strike, what's known as a call for fire. It follows prescribed steps to make sure the rounds hit the enemy, not friendly troops. We had done this training in AIT, but had to do it again anyway to make sure we still remember how to do it correctly. You have to read a map and from certain waypoints – specific spots that were precisely established locations – you figured out where you were and where you want the artillery to hit. Then, you call it in, using a specific format over the radio. It's not that hard to do, but it's just a school to check up on your knowledge and skill level. Before we could get to the call for fire, though, we had to quit the training, because another company got attacked and we had to make an air assault to help them. When we arrived, the VC were still there and we had a little contact, but they broke it off and ran, so it wasn't much of a fight.

On August 6, we were a reactionary force based at LZ Ollie, ready to go help, if someone gets hit by the enemy. In the late morning, we made an air assault on the beach and swept a village. We were back at LZ Ollie by the afternoon.

On August 7, while up in the mountains, we ran across some VC in bunkers. One of the bunkers had a machine gun in it. The soldier who spotted it came back to report to the captain what he had seen. The captain told him to knock out the bunker and capture the VC alive. Needless to say, they didn't capture any alive. One of the rules of engagement is that you weren't supposed to have a round in the chamber of your weapon while out in the field. It was about the stupidest thing I had ever heard. If I had followed that rule, I wouldn't have come home alive. I always had one in the chamber when I walked on patrol. We all did. I also had it on full automatic. Actually, that wasn't always true. I had my reflexes and weapon oiled so much that I could hit my safety with my thumb and flip it to full automatic at the same time I pulled the trigger to fire. The first thing that moved got a burst of 20. If you don't believe me, you can ask those three dead pigs that ran out of a bush beside me and almost gave me a heart attack. I had birds fly out. I had animals running out in front of me. I just shot them. It was a lifesaving reaction. My life, not theirs.

Around August 8, we got a huge surprise, a good one – orders for immediate R&R in Hawaii! I rushed to An Khe and called my

Mother who called Beth in Phoenix and told her to meet me in Hawaii. This happened really fast. There was nothing holding us back this time.

# CHAPTER 10

BEFORE I TELL the story of our R&R, I want to share the story of how we met and got married. This chapter will be told by Beth, both the part about how we got married and the R&R, because she went through a lot of it that I didn't experience. Here's Beth.

All right, 54 years was a long time ago – over 54 years, because that's how long we've been married – but I still remember that time pretty well. I first saw Dennis probably in the spring of '65. We were both students at Eastern New Mexico University, which is in the town of Portales, about 20 miles southwest of Clovis. Portales is even smaller than Clovis, maybe half the size.

One day, I was walking through the gym with a friend of mine and I looked in the gym and there was the head of the PE Department playing badminton with a young student.

I looked at my friend and said, "I really liked that guy's legs. He's got good looking legs. Do you know who he is?"

She answered, "Yeah, he was my dance partner" in some class that they had to have.

I responded, "I'd love to meet him." I don't know if you'd call that love at first sight or just legs at first sight, but it was a good start. The fact that my friend coincidentally knew Dennis made things a little easier. At a college with only a few thousand students, it wasn't too surprising.

So, we went on over to the campus union building and we're having sodas and visiting with other people. The whole time, I kept my eye out for that badminton player. Finally, I saw him come in, so I tapped my friend's arm and she looked over at him. I don't know if she waved at him or if he waved at her or what, but he did come over to the table. My friend introduced us to each other and we visited a bit, as my friend smoothly withdrew to talk with other people.

I said something about, "I live in Clovis."

And he said, "Oh, I do too."

One of us, maybe me, maybe Dennis – let's say it was Dennis who said, "Well, we need to get together sometime."

I said, "I'd love to," and we arranged to have a date, which I think it was maybe the next night. I told him, "Now, I live out of town a little way" and explained where I lived.

Dennis replied, "Oh well, that's a long drive," which was not the most flattering response that a girl wants to hear, especially in the first few minutes of meeting a guy, but I didn't let it bother me too much.

So, I offered, "Well, I'll meet you halfway." But Dennis was more gentlemanly than his initial reaction suggested and he did come all the way out to pick me up that night for our first date. And, he was only 15 minutes late – that was the earliest late he ever was, all the time we were dating.

Dennis always had something going, he was always busy. He was still in school, working, and we did a lot of things together. On our first date, we went bowling and then went over to some friend's house and played cards. We dated just like all normal people, except when would we go to the drive-in theater, Dennis would sleep all the way through it. This was because, besides running his archery shop, he also worked on the railroad and a lot of times he'd have to go to work at midnight or something like that. All this in addition to his school course load and, now, spending every possible minute with me.

The fact that he gave me so much time and attention, regardless of his other schedule demands, made it clear how he felt about me. Likewise, I wanted to be with him constantly. I knew from the start, deep in my heart as well as on the surface of my goose-bumped skin and flushed face, that he was the man I wanted to spend my entire life with.

We did a lot of things with his parents. We would go up to their cabin outside of Las Vegas, New Mexico, which was almost 200 miles from Clovis, near the Santa Fe National Forest. In the winter, we'd sled on Coca Cola discs and go up and down the road and slide to see who could make the best times – just all kinds of stuff, always having fun together.

I got into archery with Dennis. He and another guy had an archery shop where they fixed bows and made arrows and sold everything related to archery. It was a passion of his and I was happy to share it. I'd hang out in the shop with them and learned about all the equipment, products, and the sport, in general. Dennis taught me how to shoot and I quickly came to enjoy it as much as he did.

We dated the rest of the spring, all summer long, and then through the next fall. Dennis was still in school the first semester. I remember, at the end of the semester, I fractured a vertebra in my neck on the trampoline and I had to go over to find Dennis. He was taking a test on keeping score in bowling. The professor told me I had to come in and keep the official score. So, I sat there with a broken neck and kept score. Also, that night, Dennis had already done the paper we both had due for class and I hadn't written mine yet. So, he just changed his around so that I could use it, too, since I was having difficulty due to my neck. It was basically the same paper, but it was written differently. That was how Dennis was, always finding a way to help me when I needed it.

When the second semester was approaching in the wintertime, Dennis was ineligible to go back to school, because he had a GPA of 2.95 and he had to make a 3.0 to go back to school. He had missed the 3.0 only because of a poor grade on that paper.

I ran into the professor before Christmas and he asked me, "Who wrote this paper for you guys?"

I replied truthfully, "Dennis wrote it."

He didn't really believe me and said, "It's a really good paper, but it's only one paper and the other one's just been changed."

I repeated, "Well, Dennis wrote it."

He went on to say, "Whoever wrote it deserves an A and the other person will get an F."

My response was, "Okay, Dennis wrote it. He gets the A and I get the F."

He just shook his head and said, "I'll tell you what, that must be true love."

He didn't change Dennis' grade, which might have made Dennis eligible for the next semester, but oh well. Later, Dennis used to play a lot of golf with this old professor, he seems to still think to this day that I wrote the paper and Dennis didn't.

I did my student teaching in the second semester of that year and graduated when that was over. Dennis was still working the railroad and at his archery store. We were shooting a lot of archery, too. I was living at home and he was living at his home, but we spent as much time as we could together.

We started talking about getting married when I was doing my student teaching and Dennis was out of school. We got engaged in March and decided we would get married sometime soon, although we weren't sure exactly when yet. His Mom and I met and went over to Lubbock – about an hour and a half drive each way – and went to a jewelry store that Dennis and I had looked at once before. I knew exactly what kind of a ring I wanted and we found the wedding ring and the engagement ring right away. We might have also picked out the ring for Dennis or he might have gone back later and picked out his wedding ring, I don't remember any more.

Before we decided on the wedding date, we were waiting for him to receive the papers saying that he had been selected to go into the army. Friends and neighbors had received theirs, so we expected that he would get his sometime soon. We didn't want to make such a big decision until we had all the information.

My mother and I talked a lot about it. Dennis and I were, of course, always concerned that, if Dennis were drafted – and we knew he would be – that there was a chance he might be killed in Vietnam. And we talked about the advantages or disadvantages of being married, if that happened. There weren't any advantages to him being killed. Definitely none. But, we just really had a hard time making up our minds about if and when to get married.

Finally, I talked to my mother one day and she said, "Do you want to be married to this man, to have some time with him as a married couple?"

I answered with certainty, "Yes, I really do."

Her answer was pretty clear, "Then, get married."

It was now clear in my mind, too. "Okay, we'll get married!"

Dennis and I talked it over and it was finally decided – we would get married.

I graduated from college around June 1st or 2nd of 1966. My sister, Sue, had her wedding scheduled for July 30, so we had to plan around that. We chose June 16, a little over two weeks after I graduated from college. Dennis and I wanted as much married time as possible before he left, knowing that it would never be as much as we hoped. Every woman wants her wedding to be special in every way, every detail. It's her big day, her once in a lifetime. With such little time, I knew I didn't have that luxury of intricate planning of every little thing. So, I had to find my own way of making the day mine, something to make it personally meaningful. I decided it would be to wear my mother's wedding gown for my own wedding. My sister also wore our Mom's wedding gown for her wedding. We both wore the same maid of honor dress at each other's wedding. That made it very special for each of us – connected to each other and to our mother.

Despite everything, our wedding was a happy day. It felt so much better for Dennis and me to be married. I had a wonderful man as my husband, just like I had always dreamed.

I started teaching school the middle of August. It was my first job out of college, which was exciting and a little scary. I was happy to have Dennis with me to listen to my stories (and a few gripes) and share my excitement and small fears. He was very good about being supportive and encouraging, a perfect husband and friend. Of course, we both had something else looming over us. Talking about my day at school was kind of a distraction from what we knew was coming too soon.

On my birthday, Wednesday, August 31 – the day I turned 22 and 72 days into my marriage to Dennis – I went to the bus stop at the post office and met Dennis and his Mom and Dad. My dad was postmaster, so he was there, too. We said our goodbyes, all keeping as dry-eyed as we could, then watched Dennis get on the bus and take off for Amarillo, Texas, on the way to Fort Bliss and basic training.

It was hard to see the man I loved ride away, but I was happy for the year and a half or so that we had spent together, almost every single day. I was happy that we were husband and wife. And, most of all, I was happy for the love we felt for each other.

I think I took a bus down to El Paso one time to see Dennis at basic training and drove down there another time, but those were the only two times I saw him while he was at Fort Bliss. I wasn't able to visit him while he was at Fort Polk, but saw him when he came home for the Christmas break. Then we had about a month between his training and when he left for Vietnam. When I list our time together like this, it doesn't sound like much, but we made the most of it and it felt both quick and like it would never end.

Once Dennis was in Vietnam, the only time I knew I would see him was when he had R&R in Hawaii. It would be about in the middle of his tour. The only way I might see him sooner was if he was wounded so badly that they sent him home, which I didn't want to happen. So, Hawaii it would be.

School had gotten out at the end of May, and we still really didn't know exactly when we were going to have an R&R or if we even were. So, I went to Phoenix area where my sister and her husband, Artie, were living. He was a fighter instructor pilot at Luke Air Force Base. I went out there to stay with her, because she was quite pregnant, due either at the end of July or beginning of August.

It was really, really hot in Phoenix. If you've never been there in the summer, I can tell you that it's miserably hot, especially for pregnant Sue. I don't know how anyone can live there full-time. We went to the movies a time or two just to get out of the house and go somewhere that it was cool. Movies like Barefoot in the Park, You Only Live Twice, To Sir With Love, and Thoroughly Modern Millie were popular that summer – I wasn't in the mood to see The Dirty Dozen or Divorce American Style – but the air conditioning was even more popular. You couldn't go swimming. They had a swimming pool in the complex, but it was too hot to stay out there for any time at all. I'd go to the pool at about 10:00 or 11:00 at night – a lot – just going out there and getting wet and cooling off helped a lot – it was a lifesaver for Sue who was carrying a big belly.

The baby arrived on August 4. At the time, I thought it was at least a month before I'd be leaving for Hawaii, but it turned out I could only stay to help her for a few days before we got the good news of the R&R.

I don't know if my sister and new nephew got out of the hospital on the 5th or the 6th, but it was one of those two days that she brought the baby home. I slept downstairs the next few nights, so the baby wouldn't wake me up. A couple nights later, the phone rang unexpectedly quite early, maybe 5:00 in the morning. I heard Sue answer, then saw her come to the top of the stairs. She gets a little worked up at times.

She sputtered excitedly, "Beth, Beth, Beth."

I said, "Yes, what's the matter."

She finally got out, "Max, Max is on the phone. She wants to talk to you."

Max is Dennis' mother so, of course, the first thing that probably went through her mind – and also mine – was that something had happened to Dennis.

I got to the phone and Max said that Dennis had called and had gotten his R&R papers for Hawaii. I was so relieved and thrilled. She told me the day he was supposed to be in. I don't remember right now what day it was, but I needed to make reservations on a plane immediately. Max said that Dennis thought that I could get a cheaper rate because he was military, but we didn't care about that. Artie took me to the airport and got me on the first plane headed to Hawaii.

Artie helped us a lot here. With Dennis getting army wages and me as a first-year teacher, a trip to Hawaii was too much for us to afford. My teaching salary was only $3,200 a year, the equivalent to about $26,000 in 2021, so not a lot. Dennis' pay was only $2,135 a year, not including combat pay and other add-ons, or the equivalent of about $17,400. We weren't poor, but we weren't rich either and we hadn't had a chance to save any money yet. So, a trip to Hawaii was a stretch for us. Fortunately, Artie was able to use his rank to get me official orders allowing me to travel by military aircraft to Hawaii. This wasn't improper. Family members were allowed to fly "space-available" on military flights. Artie was able to ensure me a seat, though, keeping me from getting bumped onto the waiting list.

Before I had left Clovis to go out to Arizona, I knew that Dennis would need a few things for the R&R. So, I included in my suitcase the winged shoes that he liked, a couple pairs of pants, and Southwest shirts – you know, just stuff that he might prefer to wear instead of his uniform.

I met a lady on the plane who was going to Hawaii to meet her boyfriend for R&R. She told me where they were staying and that she had made reservations already. I hadn't had the time or thought to make any reservations. I didn't even know if there would be rooms available, where to go once I arrived, where Dennis would arrive – anything. I was just playing it by ear. Fortunately, she invited me to tag along with her.

When we got there, I was able to get a room. It was like a cabin, with lots of glass around it, tile floors, one big room with a little kitchenette. It had a bed that was almost like a bunk bed, but it wasn't two levels, it was just one big bed. I thought, well, this'll be okay. Next, I knew I needed wheels, so I rented a red two-door, Corvair convertible. I was going to pick Dennis up in style.

I then got on the phone and started making calls to the place I had learned the buses would come into. In what I was learning was the army style, they couldn't give me the right information with just one call. Eventually, they told me that the bus would come in about 4:00 the next morning. I stayed awake pretty much all night, so I wouldn't oversleep and leave Dennis stranded at the terminal.

I drove to the bus terminal the next morning and got there early, before there were any buses. I just sat in the car and watched. At well after 4:00, I finally saw a bus pull up and another one coming and another behind that. I got out and went over to a big building where the buses were arriving.

Inside, there was a long hallway that went way back with women just stacked on each side, waiting for their husbands. I was at the very back, because I didn't have any idea if Dennis would be on these buses or not. I really didn't know what day or time he was coming in and none of the army folks could tell me. So, I watched and hoped as three busloads of men got off and were greeted very happily by their wives. And I thought, how wonderful, they're getting to see their husbands. It made me even happier that I was about to see mine. As more and more men went by, though, that happiness gradually faded as I began to realize Dennis might not get there that morning.

At the very end, there were two other ladies besides me standing in that hallway. Over the PA system came the announcement, "Would Mrs. So-and-so and Mrs. So-and-so please come to the information desk." Both of them looked at each other and went over. I followed behind, so I could find out what was going on. I couldn't hear what the clerk told them, but each of the ladies just burst into tears. This shook me up a little. I didn't ask anyone anything. I kind of stood there and thought, well, I hope they don't call my name. And they didn't. So, I went back out and loaded into my little Corvair convertible.

To kill time, I went to Sears and bought a pair of shorts or maybe a muumuu – I bought something. Then, I went back to the little room that I had rented and hung around there, kept making calls, trying to get some clear, reliable information on when Dennis would arrive. Nothing.

The next morning, I was supposed to be there for a 5:00 bus arrival. I got there again on time and went to stand in the line and watch all those men, three busloads of men, get off the buses and walk down the hallway. That day, all the other women's husbands came in, but I was still there. No Dennis. I started thinking that Max got the date wrong, or Dennis got the date wrong, or I got the date wrong. Maybe the month was wrong and the R&R really was in September, as we had thought. Whatever the reason, I was going to make the best of it and not get upset.

Making the best of it didn't include the Corvair anymore. I decided two days of renting a convertible was enough, any longer was going to be too expensive. So, I rented a Volkswagen Bug Beetle. That would have to be adequate style for picking up Dennis.

The third morning, I parked the little Beetle and went in and again stood in the line of women along that hallway. My hope of seeing Dennis was mixed with an expectation of possibly, maybe likely, being disappointed again.

Well, the buses came in, looking like a replay of the past two days. The first bus came in and all the men started out unloading. I watched and watched and watched. No Dennis. The whole first bus, no Dennis. Then, the second bus pulled up and the men started getting out. They came one by one down the steps, down the hallway, greeting their wives. No Dennis. The third bus pulled up. The parade of men unloading began again and I was still standing there waiting. I was thinking, surely he's going to get off of this one. Right as the last five or so people were stepping down, I saw this guy get off the bus.

When we got married, he weighed 210 pounds. This guy I saw looked like him, but he was a whole lot skinnier. He had a receding hairline the last time I saw him and this guy had bleached brown hair, it was almost red, a big shock of hair going across his head. He got off the bus, pulled out a pack of cigarettes, and lit a cigarette. Dennis had never smoked before in front of me. As he started walking toward me, I decided, yeah, that's Dennis. We greeted each other with a big kiss and "good to see you." After six months of separation and three days of waiting, we were finally back together. Despite my surprise at his appearance, I was so glad to see him, hold him, and kiss him again. He was, too.

And he said, "Oh, by the way, here's so-and-so, his wife or girlfriend is coming in this afternoon and I told him we would go with him and pick her up." And I said, that's fine. This was just like Dennis, offering to help someone he had just met, even if it was a little inconvenient for us. So, we all got into the little Beetle and went back to the little apartment that I'd spent two nights in.

When we got there, Dennis said to the guy, "Why don't you go walk around the block a few times? We want to have a chance to visit." The guy didn't need any more explanation and left us alone for a while, so we could get reacquainted. Dennis had stopped in Guam and had picked up a fifth of Crown Royal, which we started drinking at about 5:30 in the morning. We then enjoyed ourselves for a little while until the other guy came back.

Dennis told me that, on his way to Hawaii, he saw the sun come up twice. The sun was just coming up when he left Vietnam and it was dark when he landed and he saw it come up again. Because he had crossed over the International Date Line, he saw the sun come up twice in one day, which is kind of unusual. The flights he flew to Hawaii were commercial airliners with stewardess that fed them. They even had movies on them. Most of the guys that went to Hawaii were officers and they got a little nicer treatment than the enlisted guys, so Dennis got it along with them. He wasn't complaining one bit.

Later that first day, we ended up driving around the island and went to a SeaWorld-type park where they had killer whales and different sea animals. We enjoyed that. I don't know if we went to see some friends of my Mom and Dad's that day or another day. It seems like we went to see them, but maybe we didn't. Whatever we did, it didn't really matter, as long as we were together.

I had bought a Hawaiian dress and bought Dennis a matching shirt. We took a catamaran cruise around Diamondhead one evening. They had dinner for us and drinks, a little dancing outside. We stood by the railing and watched the water and the sights.

We drove by different sites in Hawaii. It was really a beautiful place. Another night we went to Don Ho's place and Dennis was even invited up on stage for everyone to sing happy birthday to him. It was a little past his birthday and a little before mine. We thoroughly enjoyed that. We would go out and have breakfast and drank milk shakes, cream pies, anything that had milk in it. He was just determined to drink and have all that stuff.

Dennis decided that the little cabin wasn't a good enough for us to spend our R&R together. We felt we deserved the best hotel room they had. He called and got reservations at the Outrigger, the newest hotel in Hawaii, and we moved into that. It was really nice, we had a beautiful room. The only problem was that they were building a new hotel right next door to us. Every morning at 6:00, we heard loud ka-punk, ka-punk, because they were driving the big metal posts into the ground. We didn't care. We were happy.

We picked up many small bottles of alcohol – whiskey and vodka and whatever, as much as we could put in Dennis' bag among the clothes. We'd had the clothes that he had worn on the trip to Hawaii and the clothes I bought for him. I don't know now if he had packed any other clothes or not. When we packed him up to go, we put bottles of booze in every little pocket that he had on his pants and his shirt, and down the sleeves and pants, so they wouldn't break. I don't know if he was supposed to take alcohol back to Vietnam or not, but he had told the guys that he would bring back some booze for them.

We spent six days together in Hawaii. We had a wonderful time and it was so good to see Dennis and catch up on all we had missed. I still love him as much now as I did way back then, probably even more. You grow a little closer. Thinking back on that time makes me feel even closer to him.

# CHAPTER 11

THIS IS DENNIS again. We stopped at Guam on the way back from Hawaii and I bought about as much booze as I could. I was scared they would take it away from me when I got back, but they never searched my luggage or anything. When I got back to An Khe, I bought a case of beer and loaded it and all the booze in my pack and took it to the field. When I arrived at my unit, I just told the guys in the platoon to lineup and I just passed out beer and whiskey in little pint bottles. I kept a couple for me and the guys were very thankful.

I was 24 and I was one of the older guys over there. Most of them were 18, 19, 20 years old. Their R&Rs were Bangkok or Taiwan or someplace like that. They came back with the clap and broke. They never brought any money or booze back. So, they were tickled to death to get the stuff I brought. Some of the sergeants in the company CP came by and I gave them some booze. I don't know that I gave any to the lieutenants and I don't think I gave the captain anything. They could get whatever they wanted. I always tried to take care of the soldiers – the enlisted men, the grunts – and they were very appreciative and it's something that I enjoyed doing and they enjoy getting it.

We were at LZ Two Bits, which was on the south side of Bong Son. It was a smaller base, maybe a quarter mile from end to end, including a runway. 1st Cav had a forward command post there, which meant a small element of the division headquarters that was located closer to the front lines.

In my letters home, I wrote about an experience, but didn't tell the story the way it really happened. The real story is this. We were supposed to go on listening post on the night of August 24. The LP was by a village and, in the village, my fire squad said that there was a whorehouse where they wanted to go for some fun. I said, no. We had a mission to perform and I couldn't have half the squad naked throughout a whorehouse if the VC showed up. If we got caught or anything went sour, we would be in big trouble. They argued that I had just got back from R&R had gotten everything I wanted. We argued for a while and I finally gave in, against my better judgment. I told him that I would sit in the middle of the room and manage the radio all night.

Well, there were six of us and one of them was a guy from Puerto Rico. Without any of us noticing, he took off and was running all around the village. The MPs caught him and took him to the captain. The captain called us on the radio and informed me that he had this guy and told us to come to the CP. I was pretty pissed off at this Puerto Rican guy and at the other guys in the squad for talking me into this fiasco. I was madder at myself for giving in. And, I admit that I was a little scared of what the captain would say and do. I quickly made the guys stop what they were doing and we hurried to the CP. Making the captain wait would only make matters worse.

We got a good chewing out and the captain said he was particularly disappointed in me. I tried to tell him all I did was man the radio, but he shut me up – he was right to do so. I was in charge of the squad and had abandoned our mission, for a stupid reason. I had made a bad choice as the leader. We were each given an Article 15 and fined $50 and I was taken off the promotion list. An Article 15 is the punishment a commander can give a soldier without a court martial. It's also called non-judicial punishment and can be used to take away rank, issue a fine – sometime a very large one – and a variety of other unpleasant things. We got off pretty easy, actually. Today, that $50 would be equal to less than $400. Sure, that's a good chunk of change, but I was more humiliated than anything else.

The captain sent us back out to finish our mission. I woke up in the morning finding the Puerto Rican guy, who was supposed to be on guard, asleep. First, you never fall asleep on guard duty, as I have mentioned. Second, he already got us all in trouble. I almost killed him, but I held back. We eventually got rid of him, kicked him out of the unit. I keep making a point that he was from Puerto Rico, because he would use that to his advantage. He'd pretend he didn't understand English unless it was something that he liked – like going to a whorehouse. If he didn't like what you were telling him, he said he didn't understand. I kept complaining about him and trying to get rid of him. At some point, the higher ups agreed with me and sent him away. I don't know where they sent him.

As for that Article 15, it didn't have any lasting impact on me. On my flight back home at the end of my tour, I carried all my official papers. They gave us our records to take to our next post. The personnel office gave me all my documents in a Manila envelope as part of the out-processing from Vietnam. When we landed in the States, I took the Article 15 out of the envelope and tore it up. That was the end of it. There was no other record of me ever receiving an Article 15.

The day after the whorehouse incident, our job was to patrol villages and guard them during the run-up to elections in South Vietnam. The goal was to keep from the VC from intimidating the villagers into not voting in a few days.

A couple days later marked six months in country for me, although I didn't make any note of it in the letters. I guess it just seemed like another day closer to going home. I wrote that we were in the middle of monsoon season and it rained all the time. It made patrolling miserable. The temperatures were highs around 90 degrees and lows in the mid-70s. Humidity was about 80%. I don't think the weather is ever good for fighting a war here. At this time, the company was conducting platoon-size ambushes. D Platoon saw some action and we had to go help them. Nothing big came of it.

On August 31, I wrote to wish Beth, her mother, and her father happy birthday, as their birthdays were close together. I also told Beth that I had lost my St. Christopher medal and asked for another one. I don't remember losing it now, but I guess I did since it was in my letter.

Yesterday was a bad day, as we were in a firefight. It didn't last long, but we took several casualties. I was all right, but two men in our company were killed and three were injured. One of those killed was the captain. He was about two men in front of me – I didn't have to walk point that day. He walked to the edge of a bomb crater to look around. Across the clearing made by the bomb, there was a camouflaged bunker and the VC shot him in the stomach and leg. The medic rushed to help him, not seeing the bunker either. He was shot in the chest and the round came out from the top of his shoulder. As soon as the medic was hit, we saw where the bunker was and took it out. Ron Coble and I rushed up to help the guys who were shot. Ron worked on the medic and I tried to help the captain. I did all I could, but his wounds were too bad and there was just no way I could save him. The captain died in my arms, his blood all over both him and me. He was married with three kids.

As I said, it wasn't my day to walk point. The point man was shot in the neck and died. I couldn't help but know that it would have been me on another day. You can't think like that though or it'll make you crazy. The fact is that some people died and others didn't and we don't know why it's one and not the other.

It was 10:30 at night before we got everybody down to an area where we could bring in a helicopter to take the wounded and dead out. We had to use our machetes to cut down a lot of vegetation to clear away a landing spot for the helicopter. The stupid lieutenant had made us circle where the chopper was going to land and, when it arrived, he ordered us to start firing in front of us, just start shooting for no reason. None of us understood why he wanted us to do that with the chopper about to land, but we obeyed his order anyway. The air crew heard the firing and took off. They don't land at a hot LZ, because if they get shot down, no one gets medevacked. It was a while before we could get him back. We didn't shoot the second time. There's no way to know if this delay made a difference in who lived and who died, but it sure didn't help. As we loaded them onto the medevac, we were told that the medic looked like he would live.

The next day, we went back up to where the firefight had been and the VC had dragged off their dead. Air strikes and artillery were called in all night and the place was thoroughly messed up when we went back in to look for VC bodies or any intel.

Early September had us back at LZ Ollie. It was raining all the time. The 2nd was the eve of the elections and we expected some action from the Vietcong to intimidate people from voting, maybe attacks against us. According to my count, we walked 15,000 meters yesterday to get back to the LZ. Two people passed out and had to be medevacked. We got our new captain and he seems to be the best one yet, but time will tell. Considering how long it took to get the last captain and the fact that his death was, of course, unexpected, getting his replacement in only two days was lightning speed, by army standards.

Despite my concerns, the night before the elections turned out to be peaceful. The only incident was that two ARVNs (Army of the Republic of Vietnam soldiers, South Vietnamese) hit a booby trap and were hurt and had to be evacuated.

We moved from LZ Ollie to LZ Pony, which is about 10 miles south of Bong Son. We were in a bunker by a M107 175 mm cannon, the largest artillery gun over there. It was built like a small tank. When that thing fired, it kicked up so much dirt and dust that I never did want to guard a bunker by a gun that big ever again.

September 7, still at LZ Pony. It's unusual to have stayed at these LZs for much time, but I wasn't complaining. Not having to go out on patrol was fine with me. The weather was good for staying in one place. It was hot, but cool when it rained. When it quit raining, it was hot again. The humidity made it feel worse.

September 6, nothing happening, still at LZ Pony.

September 8, same as above.

September 9, still the same.

September 10, it was too good to go on any longer. We were told that we'd be moving out in the morning. It was nice while it lasted. Ten days was the longest we'd secured an LZ – counting Ollie and Pony.

We got word that the medic who was shot with the captain died. I don't know if what we heard out in the field is accurate. It's what trickles down to us from somebody back in the rear, with everyone adding their own interpretations or getting it wrong along the way. Whether he died or not, I don't know, but that was the word we got. If he did die, I was sorry to hear it. It made that day by the bomb crater that much worse.

When the company was out walking, one platoon was on point – in the lead – they were followed by another rifle platoon, then the CP and the mortar platoon, and finally another platoon in the rear. This day we were not walking point, so we were behind the CP. A sergeant, I don't remember now what his duties were or his name, but he was an E-6, which was three stripes with a "rocker" underneath it, the same rank as a squad leader or some platoon sergeants. Maybe he was the supply sergeant or armorer or something else like that. He was a big-headed Black guy and really funny – I just remembered this the other day – and we were walking through the jungle and he had his M16 and was strumming it like a guitar. He was singing, "What the world needs now is love sweet love," (the Top 10 Jackie DeShannon hit from a couple years earlier) as we walked through the jungle. It just cracked us up. He was so funny. But, he didn't ever have to walk point.

We had set up at a position by the sea. Our platoon had to go on patrol and, you guessed it, we had to climb a mountain. The second day, another platoon would go on patrol and we would get to stay and guard the perimeter – and maybe have a chance to go swimming.

It turned out that we did not get to go swimming. We discovered some graves, which the other platoon had to dig up.

On September 14, we made an air assault to the top of a mountain and walked down it to set up in the valley below. A day or two after that, nine of us were sitting out on an ambush and it turned into a nightmare. We set up our ambush and had no trouble until about 3:00 in the morning. I was on guard when they started firing artillery rounds down the valley. They were "walking" the rounds down the same trail we were ambushing. The impact of the rounds started getting closer and closer to us. I woke up the sergeant and he radioed the CP and notified them that the rounds were getting close and to the call it off. We could hear the rounds exploding and coming down the trail. As they got really close, we jumped in the bushes and anything we could get behind. One guy jumped on top of me and I told him to stay where he was. He told me, in no uncertain terms, heck no and rolled off. We were in the fetal position with our hands over our heads. One landed pretty much on top of us, so close that one guy got powder burns from the explosion – Freddie, the Mexican guy from Lubbock. One guy got hit with shrapnel just above the boot and it shot all the way up his shin and out his knee. I told Beer Belly – that was what we called our machine gunner – to patch him up, while I called for a medevac. Beer Belly got sick from the sight and said he couldn't do it.

I jumped over him and started putting a field bandage on the guy's leg. The field bandage is a gauze pad about the size of both of your hands together and has two strings off each side, which you would take and wrap around the body part and tie up on top of the pad, where it would put pressure on the wound. I had what I thought was one of the strings and was pulling on it. The guy was screaming and I told him to shut up, that he had just gotten a free ticket back home. I asked for someone to light a match so I could see what I was doing. When they lit that match, I saw that, instead of the string, I had his skin and was pulling on it. I said, "Sorry," and grabbed the string. It took four field bandages to cover his leg. Each soldier carried at least one bandage and we would use the wounded person's bandage first. Medevac came and took away both of the wounded. What saved us was that the shell hit so close that most of the shrapnel flew over us. The next day, we found out that they had to amputate the guy's leg at the knee. Later on, we found out that they didn't have to, which is another example of not being able to trust the word we received from the rear.

The people who were firing those rounds were South Vietnamese with an American lieutenant as an observer and advisor. The Colonel came out to visit us and said that an investigation was taking place and that someone would hang for what happened. I'm not sure any of us believe anyone would ever get punished for what happened, especially an officer. Maybe he would at least not get a medal. It's bad enough fighting the Vietcong without having to dodge your own artillery.

On September 20, I was made squad leader, which meant I'd make sergeant soon. This was less than a month after being taken off the promotion list, but I didn't point that out to anyone. We got a new platoon leader, a 21-year-old lieutenant. We also got a new platoon sergeant, who was really stupid. He couldn't even read a map or do a bunch of other stuff, which he had to know to do his job. He didn't know a thing. The lieutenant was young, but I thought he would work out.

There were two guys who received divorce papers from their wives. One had been married for two years and the other one had been married for one month longer than Beth and me. It was really a shock to them to get those papers. As I've mentioned, everyone takes this news differently. These two guys took it pretty hard. I felt badly for them and it made me even more grateful for Beth.

On September 27, I wrote that about five or six days earlier, we made an air assault and set up on a small mountain by An Lao. We were running day patrols and night ambushes in An Lao Valley. The 3rd Platoon went on the first ambush and had VC walking through their ambush site all night long. They killed six, wounded one, and captured one, but they had one killed and two wounded I think by their own mortar rounds coming in. The next night, 2nd Platoon went out and had about the same results, but nobody was killed. The following night, I was squad leader and it was my turn to go on ambush. The captain said that a new lieutenant had heard about these ambushes and wanted to go. It's never good news that some officer wants to tag along on a mission. They almost always have the least combat experience of anyone in the patrol, yet the highest rank. By the first criteria, they should do what they're told, but by the second they're in charge. Some officers get this and are willing to learn from even the privates they're with, even more so from the sergeants. These are rare. Most feel they should share their unwelcomed opinion whenever a tactical decision is to be made. I'd have to see which kind this lieutenant was. We waited and waited for this lieutenant to get ready. Maybe he was reading the operator's manual for the M16. Finally, he showed up and we headed out.

It was real dark and rainy, so dark that we were holding on to the web gear of the man in front of us. We got about 700 meters when we walked into the enemy. When I say that we walked into them, I mean that literally. They were coming down the same trail that we were going up. I was squad leader and was the third guy back. The guy on point ran into the first VC chest to chest. We bounced off of them and the point man got one shot off before his gun jammed. We were all laying in the mud, listened to the enemy talking. I'm sure they were listening to us talk, too. Our adrenaline was running really high at this point, but we stayed calm and reacted like we knew we should. The lieutenant was a little panicky, though.

The lieutenant asked me what we should do, which was good. I told him to call the "old man," which is the captain, and tell him that we'd made contact. The lieutenant did so and the captain said to continue our mission to the location we had been assigned. I told the LT to go on ahead if he wanted, but the enemy was still in front of us talking. I said to call back and tell the captain we're dropping back 300 meters and setting up our ambush there. I said to give the captain those new map coordinates. I was happy to see that the LT did as I had told him to do. The old man was okay with the plan, too.

We dropped back and put a flare across the trail and hid in the bushes. He heard them going around us. It wasn't long before they came back up the trail, trying to attack us from the rear. Coming back up the trail, they tripped our flare. Well, they didn't know where we were and, when they ran, they ran right over the top of us. We were shooting them as they ran over the top of us. It was like a big clown act, except with bullets. It was kind of funny, but scary at the same time. That lieutenant never went on another patrol.

On September 29, we were manning the perimeter and another platoon was on patrol not far off. They hit a booby trap in the really thick jungle. We watched as the medevac hoisted the injured out of the jungle on a stretcher. In thick vegetation like that, when the casualty can't be moved to where the chopper can land, the Huey hovers over the location and the air crew lowers a stretcher through the trees on a motorized pulley. Sometimes a medic lowers down too, to strap the guy into the stretcher. They first flew the one who was hurt the worst into the perimeter, where he could be given more thorough first aid, then went back to get the other two. After getting all three out all by stretcher and flying them to our perimeter, they loaded up all three and took them to the hospital. The one who tripped the booby trap was hurt really badly. The other two had only leg wounds.

That brought September to a close, seven months through my time in Vietnam.

# CHAPTER 12

THERE ARE A few things I want to cover that weren't written about in the letters. They are still important moments in my year in Vietnam and have to be included.

I want to add one more story about Beth. I don't remember exactly when it happened, but Beth said it was after R&R sometime. I was back at An Khe and they closed down the PX to anyone but our company. Only our company was able to go in a shop during this time. I suppose they did that for different field units to give them the chance to get what they needed, since we had such limited opportunity to shop. I went to the PX and bought Beth a double strand of pearls that she still has to this day. It made me feel really good to get her something nice. For most of the year I was in Vietnam, I didn't have any chance to get her nice gifts. Vietnamese kids didn't have pearl necklaces to sell to us. So, this one time meant a lot to me and, I think, to her as well. Most of the guys were buying things for themselves, but I didn't even think of that. My only thought was to get something special for my wife. The fact that she still has them tells me that the gift was as special to her as it was to me. Over fifty years later, it's something I had to make sure to include in our story.

The next thing that wasn't in the letters is something that feels kind of strange, kind of hard to talk about. It was my experience with God while I was over there. I touched on religion and faith a little before, but these are two particular moments that I want to go into more detail about.

I prayed every night and also when we had church services. A chaplain would come out to the field sometimes and hold a service for anyone who wanted to join in. Not everyone did, but we had a good number each time. I did every time I could, when I wasn't on patrol. I also went to services back in the rear when I had those opportunities. I want to describe something different from praying and services, though, something that happened to me.

People say, well, you have all kinds of different experiences and everything, but this was mine and it was unusual because I felt like I talked to God, that He was actually with me and I spoke to Him. It was a one-on-one conversation and He was an actual person, or however you'd describe Him. It didn't happen when I was scared or out of fear or anything, but when I was more at ease.

We were in this one place, I don't remember where, waiting for the helicopters that were going to pick us up. I was sitting on this log away from the other soldiers and, all of a sudden, I felt like God was right next to me, in spirit or whatever, that there was a presence there that made me feel like He was at my side, ready to talk just to me. I got to talk to Him individually. That's the best way I explain it.

I thanked Him for everything that he'd given me, especially Beth. I thanked him for giving me such a wonderful wife and for all that he had given to both of us and everything like that. I never did really talk to Him about protecting me and watching over me. The only thing I can really tell you I asked Him for was to let me be the best I could be and do the best job that I could do. I like to think those prayers were answered.

It happened more than once. I believe it happened twice that I really felt like I sat down and talked to Him. It was a strong presence of Him there in those two different times. It's kind of hard to explain to people. It's not embarrassing, but they just kind of look at me like, well yeah, they thought I kind of went off the deep end or something. It wasn't anything like that, though. It was real, whether people believe me or not. For people who do believe me – and I don't really care if anyone does – maybe knowing that this happened to me might affect their own view of God and their relationship with Him. Maybe there are others who have similar experiences, maybe other soldiers, and hearing that it happened to someone else will reassure them that their experience was also real. I have no doubt that mine actually happened as I remember it. It was too strong a feeling to have not been the truth. A lifetime later, I still can see it as clearly as the days it took place. It still makes me feel a closer connection to God.

It did affect me a little bit when I came back home. I was raised in a church and so was Beth. We went to services every Sunday. After those experiences, going back to church was a little different. I felt, well, why do I need to dress up and go to the church to talk to God when I could talk to Him more directly and personally on a log at an LZ in Vietnam?

When I had "church" out there in the boonies in Vietnam, it felt like God was riding next to me a couple of times and I was able to talk directly to Him. And when I prayed it was more like just thanking Him for what He'd done for me and everything else that was good in our lives. It was more personal and it touched me more. So, I had a little problem with church after that. Some of the best "church services" I ever had was when I was fishing, going down to the lake with the sun coming up and lighting the trees on the shoreline and just other beautiful places like that. It was moments like those that made me think of God and feel close to Him more strongly than in a physical church.

I don't know that if these two experiences happened in the first part of my tour over there or during the second half or one in each. Whenever they happened, they were big moments that changed how I feel about God and so it's important for me to include them and describe them here. It would seem to be a major omission to leave them out and not have a complete story of what happened to me during the war.

Stories about walking point bring back memories that I don't know if I put in any of the letters or not. One time on point, I was trying to hack my way through the jungle with my machete and, of course, I had a pack on my back. As I went underneath a tree limb, I hit the limb with the pack. To my surprise, the limb was just full of ants and the ants fell off the limb on top of me. I had to yank my pack and my shirt off and beat the ants off. It wasn't funny at the moment, but it is looking back. It might have also been funny to the other guys in my squad. Naturally, I had to be quiet while all that was going on, so as not to let the enemy know we were there. The other guys couldn't laugh at me too loud either. Stuff like that happened all the time.

There's another thing I remember now that I haven't run across in the letters. People always looked for ways to get out, to get sent home. Getting a serious injury was one way. This happened often in battle, as everyone knows. Sometimes, though, guys were willing to injure themselves on purpose, so they'd be sent home. It wasn't looked on favorably by your fellow soldiers, because you were essentially letting them down, leaving them short one more person. Some people were so desperate, they were willing to resort to this anyway.

We had one guy that I guess just couldn't take it anymore. From my understanding, his father was in the army and pretty high up. I don't know if that was true or not. When you dig in for the night, you try to find a perimeter where you're not right up against the jungle, you have some distance between you and the brush. So, if anybody sneaks up on you, you can see him. On this one night, we had a grassy field in front of us and we set up our perimeter there. It was our turn to guard the perimeter, we weren't on ambush or listening posts. We had our Claymore mines and flares set up out to our front. The foxholes were 10 or 15 yards to the side of each other.

Well, this guy was to the side of me and I guess he had nothing left inside and wanted out. He just took a hand grenade and threw it in his foxhole and held his foot out over the foxhole. The grenade blew up and severed his Achille's tendon and I don't know what all. It also lit the grass on fire. I brought in a medevac to get him out of there and, not surprisingly, the wind from the blades of the helicopter made the fire go faster. All the grass was on fire and it set fire to our Claymore mines and our flares. It was really a big zoo. He got what he wanted, though, even if it screwed us up some.

I thought this incident had already happened by this point in my tour. I tried to write home about everything that happened, but some of the stories got left out and I am remembering them now.

I also wanted to talk about something that happened on one of our visits to An Khe. They opened up the NCO club for us non-commissioned officers and had beer for us for free. We had steaks and we partied. Anytime we came back, we had big parties like that. Before going to the club, we had to change out of our field uniforms and put on clean ones with all the proper tags sewn on, including rank, name tags, unit patches, and other insignia. This particular time, I told myself, crud, I'm not spending money to do that. So, I went to the Supply office and went through the clothes rack and found a shirt that had all the proper insignia. The rank it had was the two bars of a captain and the nametag read "FUNK," so I was Captain Funk for the night.

We had a really good time at the NCO club that night. When we finished partying and came out of the club and one of the other guys said, "Well, what do you want to do now?"

I answered, "Crap, let's drive around the base. I haven't seen most of it. I don't know what it looks like."

He looked at me like I was crazy and asked, "How do we do that?"

I said, "Look, there is a Jeep right here. The keys are in it. Let's just take the Jeep." So, three of us stole the Jeep. One guy drove. I was on the passenger side where the captain always rode. The other guy was in the back. We drove around the base and looked at things. This was probably around midnight. I don't know how we did, but one way or another, we ran up on the perimeter fence. They had these great big, tall towers on a perimeter, so many yards apart with somebody in each one on guard duty.

And we were driving along the perimeter and, all of a sudden, this guy yelled at us to stop.

I told the driver, "Ah, the heck with it, keep going."

We kept going and the guard said, "Stop or I'll shoot."

I said, "Well, we might ought to stop." So, we stopped and this guy came down out of the tower.

He was a sergeant and he started yelling at me. "What are you doing out here?" He was just really, really mad.

I jumped out of that Jeep and yelled back at him, "Do you know who you're talking to, sergeant? I'm Captain Funk," and made him stand at attention and chewed him out for chewing us out.

He looked at me said, "Well, where are you from?"

I made up a unit, "2nd of the 5th," and added, "You did a good job, you did your job, now we'll get out of your hair."

I jumped back in the Jeep and I told the driver to get us out of there. We took off and brought the Jeep back to the NCO club. I guess we just left it there. It was a funny time and we all laughed about it later. We just took a Jeep and drove around. What are they going to do to us? We were already in Vietnam, they couldn't punish us much more than that, not for a silly stunt like this. I never worried about anything like that and I thought it was kind of exciting to do something out of the ordinary like that.

Funny thing, the guy who drove the Jeep got in touch with me less than a year ago and we laughed again about this story. However, we remember it differently. He thinks he was the one who calmed the sergeant down and I remember it as I just describe it. It doesn't matter, though. Fifty years since it happened, of course we'll have different memories of it. The important thing is that we both laugh about it still. We also talked about the lieutenant who got killed near me in the battle on March 20. I say lieutenant, because that was the rank he was wearing, although he had officially been promoted to captain the day before. This guy had really liked that captain and thought highly of him. So, we talked about him quite a bit. That was the only guy I've really been in touch with from our company in the fifty years.

I didn't put this Jeep story in any of my letters home and can't remember exactly when it happened. So, I'm just sticking it in the book here, because it's worth telling, but I don't know when in the timeline it happened. Same with the other things I've mentioned in the chapter.

One final thing stands out that I can remember now that I didn't put in the letters. It's the fear. We all had fear. However, looking back on this one time, the word panic comes to mind. Panic is bad in that it spreads and it's just contagious.

We were on patrol with the whole company and we were down in this ravine and going through it. I wasn't on point, another guy was. I was back, I don't know, 10 or 15 guys. All of a sudden, the guy on point ran back screaming, "Here they come, they're charging, they're charging, they're charging," and ran by us. He was scared to death. That was panic and panic takes over. Everybody wanted to turn and run, too, but we didn't. We let three or four guys run by us and I looked back at the captain. He just pointed at me and I took the point and went ahead. I was thinking, geez, I'm scared to death to find out what made them come running. We went on for miles and miles and never saw anything. What he probably saw was some VC who took off running when they saw him and he thought they were running at him.

I don't know if that guy was new to being on point or if he'd done it a hundred times. It didn't really matter. For a lot of us, no matter how long we'd been in country, suddenly there'd be a day when fear hit us. We suddenly believed that our day had come, this was the day we'd die. Death is so random in war that it didn't matter how experienced or skilled you were, an odd ricochet of a bullet could bring death. You could be doing everything right, the same way you did it every other day, and suddenly you'd be shot. We all knew it. Usually, we kept it out of our minds. But there might come a day when fear got the best of us and convinced us that our time was up. The problem with this is that it could cause us to act differently, putting ourselves and our fellow soldiers at risk. Maybe that's what happened to this point man. Maybe that's what happened to the radio operator in the big battle six months ago. I don't know. It could happen to anyone any time.

I didn't include this story in a letter, not for any reason. I didn't purposely exclude it. I probably just didn't think of it when I was writing. A lot of this stuff is coming back to my memory now, as I reread everything I wrote back then.

These were the stories I now remember that weren't in the letters. Now, we'll return to the letters.

# CHAPTER 13

IN EARLY OCTOBER, we were securing Bong Son bridge. I've decided to ask for a one-day leave to visit Artie, my brother-in-law. He was a major flying F-100s and had recently been sent to Vietnam. He was supposed to be stationed at Phu Cat Air Base, which was not too far from where we were operating, about 35 miles south of Bong Son. So, I thought I'd dropped down and be able to see him for a short visit.

Artie was older than me, 38, and had join the Air Force soon after college in 1952. He had flown during the Korean War and eventually flew 231 combat sorties in Vietnam. None of that mattered much to me. I just knew he was a good guy who was married to my wife's sister an he was the only person I knew in Vietnam, outside of my unit.

My leave was approved and I was to leave a couple days later. In the meantime, a tropical storm had swept in and it was raining all the time. It was a really big storm, one of the biggest I experienced over there. We were on a patrol and were coming down a mountain in the rain, slipping and sliding all the way down. We couldn't walk, it was so slippery, so we just slid on our rear end. Everybody was sliding down the mountain. We were laughing the whole time and it was actually a lot of fun, although we were filthy muddy from it all. A night around that time, we were sleeping in a bunker about 20 yards from the Bong Son River. During the night, the river rose and I woke up to ankle-deep water in the bunker. We had to move into an abandoned village and my new home was an empty Vietnamese hooch made of mud and straw.

On the plus side, I received a package from Bud containing a pint of bourbon and some food. I was grateful for both.

The day before my leave, I got into a little scuffle. Another squad leader had ordered some supplies for his squad, the same stuff I had ordered for mine. Only one of the orders arrived, so I offered to split it with him, but he said, no. He said he would fight me for it. I was challenged in front of the whole platoon, so I said, sure. We squared off in front of everybody, but I suggested we go where we won't be seen and get into trouble. He was 6'5", so the odds were definitely in his favor. I followed him as we move out of sight. When he turned around, I hit him in the mouth, took him to the ground, and beat on him for a while, until he finally threw me off. We fought back and forth until the first sergeant came and broke it up. I was thankful for that, as he was a big opponent and I was lucky to still be in the fight. I had him bleeding, so maybe he'd settle down and we could just split the stuff that had come in.

On October 10, I went on my leave to Phu Cat to see Artie, but he wasn't there, I couldn't find him. When I got back to the unit, there was a letter from Beth waiting for me saying that Artie had to go to the Philippines for a 10-day survival course, which explained why he wasn't at Phu Cat. Too bad I didn't find this out before I used a day of leave. I tried to not waste leave days and save them to use at the end of the year, so I could go home that much earlier. Oh well, at least it was a day out of the field.

Included in Beth's letter was my new St. Christopher medal, which was a real boost to my morale. As I've mentioned, it means a lot to me and I wore it every day. The several weeks I didn't have it, I felt an absence, like something meaningful was missing. It was a comfort to have it back, a constant reminder of my faith and beliefs.

On October 11, I was promoted to sergeant to go along with my responsibilities as squad leader. The additional respect and credibility that came with those three stripes would help when dealing with people who didn't already know me so well. Beth and I would also welcome the pay increase.

The next day, we moved to LZ Uplift. A few days later, we had a little contact with about 20 Vietcong. They ran as soon as they saw us. One was taking a pee. He never finished.

About a week and a half after moving to LZ Uplift, I started running a fever. It was off and on, but never happened when I was in a place with a medic, so it could be checked. We ended up at LZ Ollie and, while there, I had the doc check my temperature. It was 103, so I was sent to the 75th Medical where they kept checking my temperature – which didn't seem like the most thorough medical treatment. Sometimes my temperature was normal, sometimes it was in the 100s. They thought it was malaria. But weren't certain. They gave me some medication for malaria. anyway. It seemed to help.

On October 20, I wrote to Beth that I thought she might find it interesting how the South Vietnamese made the VC talk. I witnessed this on patrol and thought it was really pretty neat. The ARVN interrogators were supervised by Americans. The techniques they used, they learned from the Americans. We circled a village by the sea and the South Vietnamese National Police came through and searched it. They caught two suspected VC and, of course, the two of them denied they were VC and wouldn't talk.

The police took them to the beach, tied their hands behind their backs, and separated them. They would ask them a question, which they wouldn't answer. The police then grabbed the guy by his hair and slapped him over the ear as hard as he could. This was followed by a knee in the back and a judo chop to the Adam's Apple. They would ask the question again and the guy still wouldn't answer. So, this led to the water treatment. We were sitting on a wall, watching this stuff and the American advisors told us to get out of there, so we wouldn't see what was done. We just laughed at them and didn't go anywhere.

They held the guy on his back and one of them pulled a cloth over his mouth, forcing it open. They then filled a three gallon can – or maybe it was a five gallon can, it was a big can – with salt water, which they poured in his mouth real slow. While they did this, another guy would squeeze his stomach, so he would have to swallow the water. He eventually passed out and they brought him back and asked more questions. They did this over and over and the first guy passed out twice. The third time, he actually drowned, dead. Then, they started on the second guy. After the first time, he came up from them holding him down and started talking and pointing very excitedly. He didn't seem to want to go through that again or end up like his buddy. I think this is what they all call waterboarding.

Americans tried to make us leave so we couldn't witness the methods used, but it's not like any of us had any objection to what was being done. I don't know if it's officially considered torture or if it's technically illegal, but if it resulted in information that would save the lives of American soldiers or help us end this war sooner, we were all for it. We didn't condone war crimes, of course, but it just wasn't for us to judge. That's what the military lawyers are for and they seemed to have okayed it. I believe this kind of treatment was then, and maybe still is, part of what we put our own troops through during survival training. If so, I can't see how it would be considered torture or illegal. In any case, it resulted in getting plenty of good information that wouldn't otherwise been volunteered. Since the guy gave up a lot of intel, he must have been VC, after all.

On October 24, a couple days after I originally went to see the doctors, they finally diagnosed that I had malaria. They shipped me to Qui Nhon where I had a stay in the hospital. The hospital was pretty nice. We had beds with mattresses, plus clean sheets and pillows! It might sound strange that I was excited about mattresses, clean sheets, and pillows, but those were the height of luxury for a grunt soldier in Vietnam. The food was good, as it was the first real meal I had eaten in four days. It could have been peanut butter and jelly and I would have loved it. There was also air conditioning! Can you imagine air conditioning? I was in heaven and didn't want to leave any time soon.

My temperature went up again that afternoon and they made me take a cold shower for 15 minutes. I cheated and turned on the hot water, just a little. I didn't want to cool down too drastically and have them send me right back out into the field. I needed at least one more meal. After 15 minutes, I went back to the nurse and she took my temperature again. It was still high. She pointed to a guy lying naked on this rubber mattress with a temperature gauge stuck up his rear. She informed me that, if his temperature went up, cold water was pumped into the mattress. Nothing about that looked pleasant.

It sure wasn't the hospital bed I had enjoyed a few minutes earlier. The nurse told me that, if I didn't want to wind up on a mattress like that, I had one more chance to take a cold shower. Apparently, I wasn't the first G.I. to try the warm shower trick. I took a cold shower this time and it brought my temperature down.

The doctors decided to run X-rays the next day. Why, I don't know, but I was willing to do it if it meant staying longer. As it turned out, my fever didn't remain low after the shower, so leaving wasn't an option. I was still running a temperature of 104, having to take a lot of cold showers. It's funny that, when you run a fever, your body is cold with chills. I wanted to cover up to fight the cold feeling, but they wouldn't let me cover up, because of my high temperature. The other funny thing is feeling cold ever in Vietnam, where heat is a constant misery.

My stay in the hospital went on and consisted of a lot of malaria checks, soup, jello, and juice. Red Cross representatives came through and asked if I needed any writing material. They were really nice. After five days, the doctor came by and said that, after all the tests, he was pretty sure I didn't have malaria. It was what he called "the Ding" (dengue), which he said was something like typhus, but that it was a jungle virus. It was spread by mosquitos, which are impossible to avoid in Vietnam. There was no treatment, except rest and lots of fluids.

One benefit of The Ding was that it made me quit smoking. As mentioned before, I had picked up smoking while in Vietnam and that was what Beth first saw me do in Hawaii. When I got to the hospital, I lit up a cigarette and, because of the illness, the smoking made me feel so sick I almost threw up my toenails and I quit smoking right then and I've never smoked a single time since.

I got better over the next couple days. My weight came back up to 164 pounds. During that time, some Vietnamese schoolgirls visited and gave each of us a handkerchief they had made. I was released from the hospital on November 1 and sent back to An Khe.

Instead of going straight back to my unit, I decided to take this opportunity for a brief unofficial leave. I caught a ride to Phu Cat and looked up Artie. I spent two nights there before going back to

An Khe. Artie and I recorded a tape together and sent it to the Hoy/ McDowell family. I'm sure they were happy to see the two of us together – both alive and as happy as could be expected.

I'm glad Beth received that tape, because my next letter to her described some pretty ugly stuff.

# CHAPTER 14

ON NOVEMBER 6, an ARVN camp was overrun by about 200 Vietcong. We had to go out and help them. After it was over, there were 20 dead VC, according to the body count and we don't know how many they had dragged off. Our higher ups were big on body count, because that's how they measured victory, per McNamara's instructions. I'd guess that our officers bumped the number up to include an estimate of how many dead were carried away and how many might have been fatally wounded and died later. If you added it all up, the total body count during the war was probably more than the population of Vietnam.

This ARVN camp had about five different strands of barbed wire around it with cans hanging from them, so they made noise if someone moved them. The VC cut through it, anyway, and about a platoon of them got inside, surprising the ARVN. It was pretty hectic, with some hand-to-hand combat, in addition to the shooting. Hand-to-hand combat wasn't too common, because it only happened when the two sides were right on top of each other. Guns usually kept that from happening. There were nine South Vietnamese killed and a bunch more wounded. Three Americans were wounded, but not very badly.

It was a pretty fierce battle, partly because the VC were hopped up on uppers, which they were known to do before an attack. It reduced their fear and increased their pain tolerance. We finally drove them away and, as the morning got light, took off after them, but they had disappeared somewhere. It's easy for them to get away, because they know the area better than us from living there all of their lives. And, once they get to a city, as opposed to a village, they can blend in with the other inhabitants.

The next day, we were fixing to make an air assault, when we got word that a truck convoy was ambushed by checkpoint 96. That was the same place I had been when we were assigned to secure the highway. Anyway, we immediately made an air assault to there and saw that the convoy was in danger of being overrun, so they just landed the choppers on the highway and we hopped off and started engaging the enemy as the choppers flew away. Most of the fighting was at a distance of no further than 10 yards apart from the enemy. The VC had a lot of TNT and some recoilless rifles – which are like bazookas or RPGs (rocket-propelled grenades). Still, only two of the trucks got knocked out. More probably would have been, if we hadn't arrived. We eventually beat the VC back into the bushes, where they broke up and ran. We killed 14 of them and lost only one – of course, we hated to lose even one.

I took some pictures of the carnage, but left out most of the gorier images, as some of the VC were really tore up. I took some of the pictures from the helicopter. As we came in, I was sitting in the doorway of the Huey and took pictures out the doorway. In them, you could see the convoy down on the highway and white, artillery explosions going off around the trucks. I wasn't sure if the artillery was fired by Americans or the enemy. I've got a lot of pictures like that. They're pretty neat, pretty amazing, actually. We had another mission to respond to a convoy ambush later, so I'm not certain which one the photos were from, but it doesn't really matter.

The pictures I sent home were of the NVA, which is the regular North Vietnamese Army. These are not VC, which are amateur militia, but professionally trained, full-time soldiers. We call all of the enemy VC, but there's really a big difference between these two groups. Most of the ones we fought were VC. It wasn't as common to encounter the NVA. When we did, they typically put up a harder fight. The fact that 14 of them were killed doesn't mean that they weren't skilled fighters, but that they stayed to fight longer, rather than immediately running off. That's the scary part about them, in addition to them being more skilled than the Vietcong. Fortunately, we were pretty well trained ourselves.

Back at LZ Uplift, I had to get a pay problem fixed. To do that, I had to get to the Finance Office in An Khe. To justify that trip, I needed a letter from the company clerk saying that I needed to go to the rear to sign some papers for finance. The clerk said he'd have the letter by the night of November 10, so I could go to An Khe the following morning. One thing you can always count on in the army is that they'd screw up your pay every chance they got. At the start of basic training, lots of the guys didn't get paid the first few weeks. Same with when we moved to AIT and again after going to Vietnam. This time, it was my promotion to sergeant that they got screwed up. Good thing the Finance people didn't have to fight the war. We would have lost in the first month.

For the two days while waiting for the letter, I was again guarding the Bong Son bridge with my squad. Once I had the letter, I caught a ride to An Khe. Coincidentally, they were having a USO show there, along with a steak night. All that, along with getting my pay issue resolved, made it one of the most pleasant days I had in Vietnam. That was just the start of a few pleasant days in a row.

The next day, I was back with my squad and we were moved off the bridge and back to An Khe for three days of stand-down. The company had a barbecue and I was "volunteered" to be the cook. I didn't mind at all. In fact, it was fun. Everyone made sure I was well supplied with beer. Plus, I had a quart of C&C whiskey that I had bought the day before. I mentioned to the first sergeant that I had a bottle with me and, when he got thirsty, to come see me. He took me up on that offer quite a few times and, as the night went on, he got drunker and drunker. I saw this as an opportunity – although I hadn't planned it this way – and came right out and asked him if I could go visit my brother-in-law at Phu Cat. Well, it worked, and he gave me a three-day pass.

I keep talking about going to Phu Cat. Looking back, I don't know how I got there – whether it was by a convoy or a truck or whatever. But anyway, I got there. When I arrived this time, I found Artie easily enough and he was fixing to go to a wing party and I was invited. A wing is an air force unit that's equivalent to an army brigade, commanded by a full colonel. We had steak – again – and wine (this was the air force, not the army, so it was wine instead of beer), then went to the wing lounge. I don't remember our brigade having parties or a lounge, but, like I said, this was the air force. We ate and drank anything we wanted for free and really had a tremendous time.

At the party, I met a Captain Williams and he told me that he was on alert all the next day and for me to come out and see him and he would show me the birds, the F-100s. So, I did and it was really interesting. I got to sit in the cockpit of one and he showed me all sorts of gadgets and gauges. It was pretty cramped in there, with the control stick between my knees, about 25 dials on the instrument panel, and I don't know how many switches and dials. Who could keep track of all that? Suddenly, they had a scramble and I was sitting in his seat and he needed to take off. It was pretty frantic for a few seconds. Eventually, I got out and he got in and took off. Seeing a fighter jet take off is pretty cool, especially right after sitting in the cockpit.

November 12, 1967. 100 days left in Vietnam.

Artie had gotten an audio tape from Sue. Beth was on it, also, and it was good to hear her voice. It was the best way to end these few days removed from combat.

The next day, I went back to An Khe and on to my platoon. My return to the field started with a patrol. It was through really thick jungle and we had to cut our way with the machetes. I enjoyed the time off a whole lot better. The only thing good about being back was that it was one day down, one day closer to going home to Beth and never seeing jungle again. The patrol reminded me of the time a bit earlier when I was on point and we had to get to an LZ where the helicopters could pick us up. It was really thick and I was using a machete to cut our way through. It was a real bitch getting through it. On top of the physical labor of hacking a path was the ever present worry that the noise I was making would attract the VC or just that I couldn't watch out for any enemy. The lieutenant was way in the back and he yelled for us to hurry up, as we were running late for our pick-up at the LZ, as if I didn't know that and was just lollygagging and taking my own sweet time on this pleasant jungle stroll. I had no desire to stay out there any longer than necessary and was doing my best to keep us moving. And, I was in a sour mood from the exertion and heat. I didn't need a 21-year-old with weeks of field experience getting on my ass. So, I yelled back, "If that SOB wants to go faster, get his ass up here and he can walk point." It was really quiet and there was no response. I continued to hack away. Guess what, we made it to the LZ in time and that LT must have forgot to thank me for all of my hard work.

We kept our operations relatively close to An Khe, which was fine with me. It may not have been safe anywhere in the country, but it got worse the farther north we went. An Khe was a little more south than lots of the places we went. I often wrote to Beth only something like, "Another typical day. Went on a morning patrol and set an FOB (forward observation base) at the end of the day." I didn't mind "typical days." Boring was better than exciting in this job, unlike most other jobs in the civilian world.

An Khe is a really interesting place. It's very high, about 1,400 feet, with more rolling hills than mountains. It gets lots of rain, maybe more than other places in Vietnam where we operated. I heard it was a big game paradise at one time. War has a way of screwing up things like that. The base was actually named Camp Radcliff, but we mainly referred to it by the name of the Vietnamese town where it was located, like many other sites. It was named after Major Donald Radcliff, the 1st Cavalry's first combat death. He was killed on August 18, 1965, the same month the base was established, not a good start. When 1st Cav was based there, it was the largest helicopter base in the world. That tells you what a big presence in the war 1st Cavalry Division was, which is why we were in the news so often back in the States. I'm not sure if that was good or bad for those of us who were over there.

I sent two Polaroid pictures home that were dated November 15. The guys in the photos had each written their names on the back. In one, there was SP4 Ernest Canter, SP4 Chester Alfrey, SP4 Fred Ramirez, SP4 Ron Coble, and me. The other had PFC Jose Pachen, Alfrey, Canter, SP4 Tommy Herd, PFC Kenneth Barkins, Ramirez, SP4 Robert Smith, PFC Roger Koch, PFC Ray Pickens, SP4 Pancho Ortiz, PVT Obrie Collier, SP4 Rufus Adams, and me. Honestly, I don't remember a lot of the guys in that platoon. I'm really bad about remembering names and faces. There are only about three or four guys I really remember five decades later. I don't feel badly about it. It's not that I didn't care about them or who they were. It's just the way I am, I don't have the best memory for people. I like people and don't have trouble making friends. I just don't remember them after a while. Fortunately, Beth is a little better about these things than I am.

Our platoon killed an eight-foot python snake. It shouldn't have moved when we walked by. We also killed a big bamboo pit viper. We called them the step-and-a-half snake, because that's how far you'd get after being bitten before you died. I don't know how true that was, but none of us wanted to put it to the test. The bamboo viper is about three feet long, bright green with a yellow underside. The creepy thing about them, besides how poisonous they are, is their yellow eyes. I've never seen another animal with eyes that looked like that. They are aggressive and quick to bite. So yeah, we shot it.

For Thanksgiving, we were served a special holiday dinner. The special thing about it was how especially bad it was. Looking back, I don't know why it was so bad. It sounds good to me. You'd think that anything would be better than more C rations. Maybe I was just hoping for better. In truth, the army cooks did a pretty good job on the rare occasions that we got to have a hot meal, which we sometimes could when we were at An Khe. The army knows that an easy way to improve troop morale was to serve a good meal, which didn't cost them any more than a bad meal did. Maybe Christmas dinner will be better next month.

The next day, we took over security of the highway. My squad was in charge of checkpoint 96, which was a bridge. In the following few letters, I only wrote, "Not much, more patrols," which was fine.

The 1st Cav had special Christmas patches made. I think I got 14 or 15 of them and mailed them home to Beth, my parents, and different people.

We had some ARVNs come out to our position and wanted me to go hunting with them. I don't trust any Vietnamese, so I said no. They hunted at night anyway and asked us not to shoot them. I told them, "Don't come close to us and we won't." The next morning when I woke up, they returned having killed four deer and a wildcat. It was probably an ocelot or something like that. They plugged the bullet holes in the animals with leaves and twigs, then built a big fire and put the animals on the flames until they had completely burned the hair off and scorched the skin. They cut off two hindquarters and two front quarters and gave them to me. I tried to turn them down, but they wouldn't let me say no this time. I sold three of the pieces for $2 and gave the other one to the guys, who wanted to barbecue it. I tasted it after it was cooked. It had more of a wild taste to it. It was tougher than our deer in America. There was lots of game in Vietnam – monkeys and all kinds of stuff.

On November 26, I wrote that we were drinking beer. I don't remember the story behind that, but I'm sure we were happy for it. On November 30, we were all ordered to go to An Khe to attend a going away party for the colonel, the brigade commander. I had only seen him a couple times, including when I was presented the Silver Star. None of us really knew if we were glad or sorry to see him go. We didn't hear much about his operational or policy decisions. What we did know is that we were happy to be out of the field for a little while and have some more beer and good food, better than the Thanksgiving dinner.

With the end of November, I've survived nine months of war and am really starting to look forward to getting out of here. I try not to think too much about it, although it's hard not to count down the days – December 1 was only 81 days left. I remind myself, though, that many people get themselves killed in the last month in the field. It's a strange irony and one that I didn't want any part of. I just tried to focus on continuing to do my job as I always had, keeping me and my squad alive.

Early December brought a week or so of a really hot time, action-wise. In my letters home, I said I would write more about it later, but it doesn't seem that I ever really did. I wasn't trying to avoid telling the stories, just forgot to get back to it. I mentioned that we got 30 VC in two or three days, which is a lot. In one follow-up letter, I said we did an air assault to help out a convoy that had been ambushed. It was either this one or the earlier one that I took pictures of. We also responded to a VC attack that overran an ARVN post. I guess it was these two battles when we killed the 30 VC, or maybe it was another one. I didn't really clarify that in the letters. I suppose it doesn't matter much now. I wrote that I was fine, which is the main thing Beth wanted to hear.

On December 11, I told Beth of an incident when we were building a bunker. I was drunk and fell off of it, although I didn't share that detail in the letter. I just said that I got a piece of barbed wire stuck in my elbow. The cut got infected and I had to go to An Khe to have it lanced. They gave me two shots of antibiotics, which solved the problem. Five days later, the doctor took the bandages off my arm and said the injury had healed. Good thing it kept me from going to the field during that time or it probably would have gotten worse.

The night I got injured, I was assigned the extra duty of being the brigade NCO on the night shift, until I was released by the doc to return to the field. That just meant I had to sit at this desk and answer the phone and take care of whatever their problems were. The things people called the brigade office about in the middle of the night, at least those nights, were minor and could either easily be dealt with or could wait until morning. It was easy duty for me. And gave me a chance to heal.

During this time, the middle of December, I received lots of letters and packages from different people. We were all getting a bunch of packages, because Christmas was coming and people wanted us to know they were thinking of us, which we appreciated. Beth's sorority sent me two or three little boxes containing all kinds of stuff, hot sauce and everything. I passed them out to the other guys. It was really great. I can't tell you how much stuff was in them, but I shared it with everybody and we were all tickled that we had gotten it. I went to the PX at An Khe to buy Beth a Christmas present and send it off to her.

I received word that I would be stationed at Fort Hood after my combat tour to finish my time in the army. Fort Hood is a huge army base in central Texas, between Austin and Dallas. It was as good a place as any to spend a short time. It was one of the closer bases to home, so that was good.

Mid to late December was a busy time and I went all over Vietnam. We had been in the field for a long time when, all of a sudden, we were rushed back to base camp at An Khe. There, we were put in line, told to hand in our old web gear, and got new web gear and new uniforms, all brand new and clean. We had to have all of our insignias sewn on. This took up most of a day, December 23. Everybody was saying that we were going to go see the Bob Hope show, so we were pretty excited. We knew that, in addition to Hope and his usual collection of performers, Raquel Welch was on this tour. She had just had her breakout hits that year – Fantastic Voyage, One Million Years B.C., and Bedazzled – and her cavewoman poster made her the hottest pin-up in the world. We couldn't wait to see her.

We were loaded onto C-130s and flown to Cam Ranh Bay. We checked in our weapons and were put in formation on the tarmac. There were thousands of soldiers in formation with a big stage in front of us. I somehow ended up in the front row – I was going to have a close-up view of Bob Hope and the rest of the show. A plane landed and reporters and cameras and equipment got off and set up in front of the stage. Then, Air Force One landed and President Johnson got off. He got on the stage and requested that the troops be allowed to break ranks and come close, so we could all hear him. There I was, in the front row with only reporters between me and the Commander in Chief – the guy who had sent me to Vietnam. He gave us his Christmas address, which honestly, many of us didn't give two hoots about. We had wanted Bob Hope and Raquel Welch.

One of the reporters turned around and said to me, "He is really sincere."

I replied, "Bullshit!"

He turned around and never looked back. He must have been new in country and not been very familiar with soldiers and how we felt about our Asian vacation.

When Johnson finished, he got back on his plane and took off for the next stop on his world tour. We were put on buses and they took us to mess halls and fed all of us a Christmas dinner. It was much better than the Thanksgiving dinner. We were then put back on the buses, where we sat and waited. We didn't know what we were waiting for – the army was known for making us "hurry up and wait" – until General Westmoreland, commander of all US forces in Vietnam, got on every bus and wishes us a Merry Christmas. To me, that was more impressive than listening to Johnson. At least Westmoreland was here in Vietnam with us. He was one of us.

They drove us back to the airfield and flew us to An Khe. The next day, we lined up to turn in all of our new gear, except for our uniform, and were given our old stuff back. We got on helicopters and went back to the field. And that night I was on ambush, a day after not seeing Bob Hope.

The next morning, I was coming back to the perimeter from the ambush and they flew in hot breakfast for us. The pilot was dressed up as Santa Claus. It was a really nice way to celebrate Christmas, better than all the hoopla with the president.

1967 ended with a couple of interesting items. I learned that I had been given an in-country R&R that was scheduled for last part of January. Then, on December 29th, the full company was on patrol and the point man shot a big leopard. The colonel flying overhead in a helicopter, apparently heard the shot or something and wanted to know what happened. The captain told him what had happened and the Colonel said he was going to the land and take the leopard. The captain told him that the leopard was his and there was no place to land. I don't know who wound up with the dadgum leopard. The point man should have kept it, but that wasn't going to happen once the officers found out about it. Anyway, we took pictures holding that leopard and I sent one home. It was a really beautiful animal and the picture turned out great.

We didn't have much of a New Year's celebration, nothing that I mentioned in my letters, although we might have had a little alcohol. The important thing to me was that New Year's Day marked 50 days left in Vietnam. But, who's counting?

# CHAPTER 15

THE NEW YEAR seemed exactly like the old one. It started with us back out in the field and it was raining really hard. The monotony and repetition were constant. We had really been picking off the VC lately, without getting any of us hurt. That was always good news.

I chose not to worry about the statistic of how many guys got killed in their last month and decided to actively count the days until I rotate. I drew a Snoopy on my helmet and blocked off the number of remaining days. I crossed each one off as the days passed. It made me feel better, like I had something tangible to look forward to – which I did, being home again with Beth.

I wrote to Beth that I had been assistant platoon sergeant for some time now, basically the number three guy in the platoon after the lieutenant and the platoon sergeant. Basically, that meant I had more duties with no extra pay. The army did that a lot, so it didn't bother me. With my promotion to sergeant, E-5, in September, I had risen four ranks in my first year in the army, so I couldn't complain. Usually, the senior squad leader became the assistant platoon sergeant. I had been a squad leader about three months by late December. I don't remember for sure, but would guess that I was possibly the junior of the four squad leaders. I was certainly one rank lower than what a squad leader was supposed to be – sergeant versus staff sergeant. Maybe my age was part of the reason they picked me for the position or I might have just seemed more ready for additional responsibility.

We were at LZ Ollie in the middle of the month and they let some of us go to Phu Cat to the PX. I tried to visit Artie, but he wasn't there. I was told he had gone to Tuy Hoa, which was about 75 miles south of Phu Cat and right on the ocean. I did some shopping and bought two quarts of whiskey and a case of beer for the guys in the platoon.

Back at LZ Ollie, we were told to expect to be attacked one of the next couple nights, but nothing happened, except for some automatic rifle fire, which didn't hurt anyone. Looking back, we now know that the Vietcong were preparing for the Tet Offensive around this time and increasing attacks, especially on smaller or more isolated American bases. Our military intelligence had probably caught wind of this and warned everyone. Maybe LZ Ollie wasn't a specific target or it wasn't small or isolated enough. Of course, we didn't know all of this at the time.

On January 16, we were told that we would be flown the next day to the DMZ (Demilitarized Zone), which had been the border between North and South Vietnam since 1954, when the French lost their war in Vietnam. The plan was for the 1st Cav to be based closer to the DMZ and take over the fighting there from the Marines. In the second half of January, the division repositioned into the area on the south side of the DMZ, the farthest north any army unit has been in war. The division headquarters moved from An Khe to Camp Evans on the northwest side of Hue, about 60 miles from the DMZ.

We flew from Phu Cat to Phu Bai, which was a few miles southeast of Hue. From there, they trucked us to a place called Gia Le, which was just northwest of Phu Bai. We conducted a few days of border patrol search and destroy missions, sweeping the whole area, chasing out everybody and everything. Then, the engineers came and started clearing the land and putting up tents, dirt roads, fencing, watch towers, and everything else needed to have a base. You'd be surprised what they did in two or three days. We went from nothing to an operational base in the blink of an eye. It was as if we'd always been there.

After all that, I returned to An Khe to get ready to go on my in-country R&R, which started on January 27. The next letter I wrote to Beth was dated February 6. I told her I was stranded in the city of Vung Tau on my R&R and that I had bought a tailormade suit. This was my last letter home, or it was the last one we could still find. So, the rest of the story will be from my memory. It will cover my R&R until I left the country and returned home.

My in-country R&R was in Vung Tau, which was about 30 miles southeast of Saigon, on the coast. It was a port city with piers and beaches. Of course, there were also lots of bars and clubs. I was given a room in a two-story building run by the U S army. By normal civilian hotel standards, it was nothing special. By combat G.I. standards after almost a year in the field, it had a bed and a bathroom, which was like living in the Ritz to me.

The first thing I did was buy a case of beer and hire a Vietnamese guy to take me around town. He had a horse-drawn buggy. He was pretty interesting and Vung Tau was a really pretty city. The architecture was mixed and I took a lot of pictures of the variety of beautiful buildings. The architecture reflected Buddhism, Christianity, and other religions all over the city. The guide showed me an orphanage, which was for boys only. He said that there were no orphanages for girls. He didn't immediately explain why that was or what happened to girl orphans. I didn't ask. Then, he showed me where the whorehouses were, as that was where most soldiers wanted to go. Not me, though. He explained that prostitution was what was waiting for the orphan girls. It was a sad fact and one that I couldn't do anything about, except not spend my money to support that fate.

On my third night in Vung Tau, the night of January 30, the Tet Offensive broke out all over South Vietnam. This was a major escalation of the war by the Vietcong and North Vietnamese army. It was a coordinated attack on over 100 cities and villages throughout South Vietnam and one of the largest military campaigns of the war – the largest operation conducted by either side up to that point in the war. Fighting in some places, like Hue and Khe Sanh, lasted a month and longer. In the end, about 32,000-45,000 enemy fighters were killed, depending on who did the counting. About 2,800 South Vietnamese and 1,500 U.S. and allied forces were killed. The city of Hue was mostly destroyed. Tactically, our side won. Politically, the north won, as American public support for the war took a big blow and a call for negotiations to end the war picked up momentum. But, I didn't know any of that yet.

I grabbed my gear and went to the airfield to go back to An Khe. It took a few days to get out of Vung Tau and back up north. I didn't want to go back to the field and, technically, still had time left in my R&R. As I mentioned earlier, when I first got over there, once you had 30 days left to go in country, they rotated you back from the field to the rear to start out-processing. At some point, we got a new captain who cut it to 15 days and later another new captain cut it down to seven days or ten days, one or the other. Either way, it screwed me, because I would have already been in the rear out-processing at this point. That was probably part of the reason for them giving me the R&R, who knows? It would have just about gotten me to the time for me to rotate to the rear, although not quite. So, I wasn't in any rush to cut short my R&R and go back to the field.

I knew Artie was at Tuy Hoa – not so far from An Khe – so I got a helicopter ride there and looked him up. I found him and told him that I would like for him to hide me for seven days. That would be beyond the scheduled end of my R&R and would get me back to the unit just in time for my departure from the war zone. I wasn't going to be part of the statistic that die in their last days in country. He understood and wasn't going to let down his sister or his brother-in-law. No, he was a good brother, and good friend, and a good guy. He took me to the officers' club and introduced me as his brother-in-law Sergeant Hoy and told them to give me anything I wanted. Well, I drank for seven days.

On the seventh day, Artie took me to the airport and I asked the captain on duty for a flight to Hue. He asked me for my orders and I told him I didn't need orders to get in here, so I didn't need orders to get out. The captain was adamant that I did. I looked at Artie who was a major and, therefore, outranked the captain by one rank. Artie didn't pull rank, though. He had a better idea. He asked the captain if he could use the typewriter. The captain let him and Artie typed away. I gave him one editorial suggestion, to say that I had been trying to get a flight out but couldn't, because they had been under attack. He finished typing up the necessary document and asked the captain if that would do. The captain said it would.

He wasn't convinced it was official, but couldn't argue with a major. I took the "orders" with me, figuring I might need them.

I flew to Hue, where there was still heavy fighting going on, found a helicopter to Phu Bai and, from there, another one out to our company position in the field. As soon as I got off the chopper, the guys started questioning me about where I had been and said the old man was pissed off at me. He had flagged my orders – which means he blocked me from leaving the country – took me off promotion list and the Bronze Star list. I couldn't care less about the last two things. The only thing I cared about now was leaving Vietnam and I wasn't going to let the company commander screw that up for me now. I went to the captain and he demanded to know where I had been. I acted mad and told him that I had been trying to get back, but the bases were under attack. I took Artie's orders and threw them at him. After reading them, he cooled down, said he believed me, and that I could leave in the morning. I made sure he was releasing the flag on my orders, so I could leave the country. Sure enough, the next morning I was on the chopper to An Khe to process out.

It was an enormous and long-awaited relief. Honestly, I hadn't let myself completely believe this day would come, but it was here. I had left the field for the last time and was alive. I was going to survive the Vietnam War. I was going to see Beth again.

I put everything I owned in my duffel bag, except for my dress uniform, which I was required to wear on the trip home. All the things I sent to the rear for souvenirs were gone. I had taken a sword from an NVA officer and some other stuff. Supposedly, if you tag your belongings with your name on them when they take them back to the rear, those things should be safely waiting for you when you get back there. Nope. Someone had stolen everything I had. That's not the way soldiers should treat each other, but some people don't care about that. They cared more about having a damn NVA sword that they themselves had not taken from an enemy officer, but would tell everyone they did.

I flew to the army medical facility at Cam Ranh Bay, which was about halfway between where we had been fighting and Saigon. Here they checked us for venereal disease, which was an awful job. We had to walk into the bathroom and they tell you to skin it back and milk it. If any fluid comes out that shows that you have some kind of venereal disease, you can't leave. There has to be a guy who watches you do this. That's a hell of a duty, I guess.

Then, they went through my duffel bag. They found my canteen cover that had a bullet hole through it. It was from our big battle March 20. The sergeant told me that it was usable U.S. Army equipment and I couldn't take it. The army was trying to screw me one last time before I left Vietnam.

I told him, "You see that bullet hole? I was wearing this when it went through and I'm taking it home with me!"

He was unimpressed and answered, "You see that plane out there. Do you want to stay here and argue with me or do you want to get on the plane?"

I got on the plane.

I was sitting by the window. Just being in that seat was a great feeling, but there was still some level of fear that they wouldn't let us leave yet or there'd be an attack or the plane would breakdown. I tried not to think of these things, but they were in the back of my head and caused a tightness in my stomach. I looked out that window, looking for anything that might go wrong. I saw nothing. When the door to the plane was closed, I felt more hopeful that this might really be happening. When I felt the wheels rolling us back and saw the plane pull away from the gate, I started to believe things were going right. Taxiing to the start of runway seemed like the slowest and longest ride I had ever been on. Couldn't the pilots go faster? Didn't they know we were a big target? The possibility of us returning to the gate for mechanical issues or weather or enemy attacks still existed, but was growing smaller as we turned onto the runway. The plane was packed with soldiers going home. It was really quiet, quieter than soldiers ever are. Finally, the engines revved and we picked up speed, the nose lifted, then the rear tires, and we were airborne leaving Vietnam after a year of war. There was a deafening cheer that filled the cabin. It was hard to grasp, but it was over.

# CHAPTER 16

THE PLANE MADE a few stops – Japan, Gaum, maybe Hawaii – and finally landed in Washington. I believe it was Seattle, but it might have been Fort Lewis, near Tacoma. From there, I flew via Denver to Lubbock, Texas, where Beth picked me up and we went home. Boy, it was great to be with her again. Our happiness was mixed with the exhaustion of what we had been through for the past year. It felt like a huge weight had been lifted, a weight I had been carrying for a long time. I had survived the war and made it home to Beth.

I had a 30-day leave before I had to report to Fort Hood. We went and bought a brand new blue Plymouth Fury III. What better way to celebrate my new freedom than with a new car? Beth and I went to Las Vegas for a few days of celebrating. We mostly drank and lost money gambling, but it didn't matter, because we were together. That was all that mattered. From Vegas, we went to Safford, Arizona to see Beth's brother, Bruce. Safford is a small town in Eastern Arizona and Bruce taught history and government at Eastern Arizona College at the next town over, Thatcher. He invited me to speak to his class about my time in Vietnam. On the way there, I wrecked our brand new car. We had to have it towed 500 miles to Clovis to get it fixed. Still, at least no one was shooting at me and I got to be with Beth. The wrecked car was no big deal.

When we returned to Clovis, my mother said that my army friend Ron Lewis had called and told her he was sorry to hear that I had been killed in Nam. Ron and I had been friends at Basic and AIT. My Mom let Ron know that he had heard wrong and that she would have me call him when I was home from Vegas. Like him, I had heard that Ron had been killed over there. You just can't trust any of the reports you heard in the war zone about anyone dying or surviving. I called and talked to Ron and his wife, Mary, and found out that he would be stationed at Fort Hood, also. I sure did look forward to seeing him again and catching up. It certainly was good news to know he was alive and back from Vietnam.

My brother Bob, who was three years younger than me, also came home from the military on leave and was home at the same time. He had been in the Navy for two and a half years, most recently in the Mediterranean. Dad got permission to cut down a Christmas tree, which we decorated with all the trimmings and put presents around. We celebrated Christmas in February. It was a real treat for the whole family. I was happy that we didn't totally miss out on the holiday together, it was just postponed a little bit.

At the end of the 30 days, I got on the bus and rode the 400 miles to Fort Hood. I stayed in the barracks with the unmarried soldiers for about two months, until Beth could join me after school was out in May.

I expected to quietly finish out my enlistment without incident. For a little while, though, it looked like things wouldn't be so quiet for us, after all. On April 4, 1968, Reverend Martin Luther King, Jr. was assassinated and three days of riots broke out in Chicago. We had to train for riot control, in case we were called to go to Chicago. They had us march while other soldiers, acting like they were rioters, spit on us and called us names. We had to respond to them without shooting. Of course, we knew they were just other soldiers, so we didn't even consider shooting them. In the end, one brigade from Fort Hood ended up being sent to Chicago, 3rd Brigade of the 1st Armored Division. The rioting calmed down the next day and the soldiers didn't shoot anyone, as far as I heard.

At Hood, Ron Lewis and I got to spend time together. We talked about getting an early out. We all knew that the reason we were drafted was to fight in Vietnam. We had done that, so why did we have to stay in the Army another half a year? The army didn't need us and we certainly didn't need the army. So, we put in for early outs. This was a way to be released from our enlistment early for some compelling personal reason. My justification was to go back to school and Ron's was to go to South Dakota and help his Dad on the farm. I thought it might work, but he didn't. I finally talked him into applying. As it turned out, his request got accepted and mine was denied. I guess they figured I could go back to school any time. Plus, I hadn't been in school when my enlistment started, thanks to that one bad grade on my paper. Who knew that would still haunt me almost two years later? At least one of us didn't have to put up with the army any longer. I was happy for Ron, but sorry to see him go. Over the decades, he's the one person from the army I pretty much stayed in touch with.

Finally, school was out and Beth came down in our new, repaired car. Within a very short time, a drunk soldier on Fort Hood slammed his car into mine. Once again, we had to have our brand new Plymouth towed to Clovis for repairs. I was starting to think it was cursed.

Beth and I rented a garage apartment in Belton, Texas, about 20 miles from Killeen, the city outside of Fort Hood. It was really nice. Although it was small, it was all we needed. I joined an archery club in Belton, so I could enjoy my favorite hobby again during my off hours. And, I made sure I had as many off hours as possible.

If it's not already clear, I was not enthusiastic about my new assignment and my remaining time in the army. The entire reason for my having an assignment after Vietnam was to complete the two years of my draft commitment. I think we all had two-year stints because AIT for some jobs was longer than for others. Two years covered everyone's AIT, plus a tour in Vietnam. I could be wrong about this rationale, but could see no real reason for the army to keep me on its payroll for six extra months. To fill this extra time, a bunch of us grunts back from Vietnam were sent to units like 1st Armored Division and 2nd Armored Division, which were both at Fort Hood. There, we counted down the days. None of us were going to stay in an extra minute, much less re-up or become lifers. With all this in mind, I came up with a strategy for getting through this dead time in the most enjoyable way I possibly could. It also gave me extra time with Beth, once she was able to join me.

At my new unit, I would make it to the morning formation. When we were reported "all present and accounted for," we would execute a "left face, forward march." In formation, we marched down to where there were hundreds of tanks. Each of us was given a rag and told to wipe down the tanks. None of us were under any delusion that we were in any way contributing to national security and combat readiness. It was obviously just busy work, a way to keep us occupied and out of trouble. There were at least a hundred G.I.s, all back from Nam. We would start wiping the tanks until the leaders had disappeared from view and then crawl under the tanks and sleep in their shade. We would take turns on the lookout. When the lookout would yell, "the lieutenant is coming," we would crawl out from underneath and get back to wiping the tanks. At the end of these totally unproductive days, we would be marched back to the barracks area, where we would be accounted for again and released for the evening. I had better things to do than wipe on tanks. After I had had enough of this, when it was clear that the army had nothing important for us to do – or nothing that I cared to do – I would make the morning formation, execute the left face, forward march, then break off from the formation, go through the barracks, get in my car. and return to our apartment in Belton.

Beth had a great time during what amounted to an extended vacation. We took the chance to go to Marble Falls, Texas, about 75 miles from Belton, where the Burnham Brothers, Winston and Murry, were famous for making the best wild game calls for hunting. It was a thrill to visit their business, see how the calls were made, and buy a few from the selection in their store. We also hunted mouflon sheep – exotic game – on their ranch, which was a rare opportunity. Beth and I traveled quite a bit around that part of Texas during this time. At the end of each day, I would make it back to base for the evening formation, then go back home.

We also went to HemisFair in San Antonio. This was the World's Fair, a huge exposition that was held in different locations around the world every few years since about 1800 and attracted visitors from around the world. In 1968, it happened to be held just two hours from where I was stationed. The grounds covered 100 acres and it had exhibits from 30 nations. It was really neat. That was one good thing that came from being assigned to Fort Hood for those extra six months.

My sneaking out went on for some time, but we knew it couldn't last forever. Finally, at one morning formation, they said, "Sergeant Hoy, you're wanted at brigade." So, they caught me. What are they going to do? Send me to Nam and make me walk point. I didn't care. When I got to the brigade headquarters, I met with a captain who asked me a few questions.

"You have three years of college?"

"Yes, sir."

"You have a silver star?"

Yes, sir."

"You know how to type?"

"Yes, sir." I don't know how to type. They were looking for someone to do a job that calls for an E-7. I was only an E-5. The person who was scheduled to be in that position wouldn't arrive for three more months. They asked if I would be interested in doing this job until I was out of the army. I said, yes. Even though this would mean the end of my daily outings with Beth, if I didn't take this job, they would wonder why I'd rather be wiping down tanks all day. It would call attention to me and I'd get caught. So, the outings would end, either way. This was the better way.

The captain took me upstairs, opened the door, and said, "This is your office and this is Private Brown, who's your Jeep driver. Any questions?" No, sir. He left, shut the door and I asked Private Brown if he could type. He said he could and I told him that was great and he and I would get along. For the rest of my time in the army, I had a job I worked from 8 to 5, delivering papers – orders, usually – to different areas on post. We'd go all over Fort Hood. I was doing something other than wiping on tanks. I actually enjoyed it. You see, I wasn't trying to not do anything for the army, I just didn't want to do anything that was stupid. In this new job, I was actually doing something that had a purpose. That was fine with me.

Finally, in August, the end of my tour in the army came. I turned in everything that had been issued to me. Then, Beth and I drove back to Clovis to get on with our lives. We were finally going to start what we have intended since meeting in the campus union building after badminton two and a half years previously. We rented a house from her parents and started a real life together. We weren't 8,500 miles apart writing letters to each other. We weren't worried that we'd never see each other again. We knew that we'd be in the same room at the end of every day, could hold each other whenever we wanted to, kiss each other whenever the mood struck us, and sleep together all night every night.

I was placed in the army reserve, but didn't have to go to any meetings or training or any kind of duty. I was just on a roster somewhere for three or four years. Being in the reserves didn't have any effect on our life and I quickly forgot I was even still in it.

I applied for college again and was accepted. The baseball coach caught me in school and said that I had one more year of eligibility left and asked if I would be interested in playing again. I told him that I found out there was more to life than playing baseball. I thanked him and told him it was time I went to school to study and graduate. I had to prepare myself for a career.

# CHAPTER 17

I WANT TO CLOSE by discussing my feelings on Vietnam and bring it up to date with all that has happened in my life since then. Just telling the story of my time in war without sharing my feelings on everything that I experienced would only be half the story, maybe the less important half. Naturally, my feelings have changed in the fifty years since then, so I'll get into how I feel about it now, as well.

I, of course, didn't want to go to war. Most people didn't, although some people did want to go. I was drafted at a time when all I wanted to do is play baseball. Baseball was my life when I was in college. As maybe you can tell, I never did things in moderation, I always went overboard. Out of high school, I earned a full scholarship to play baseball in college. I lost the scholarship due to poor grades, which was a reflection on my lack of maturity then. However, I immediately got another baseball scholarship, which is how I ended up at Eastern New Mexico and met Beth. When I played baseball at ENMU, my very real goal was to be a professional player in the major leagues. When I got into archery, I was the state champion and the Rocky Mountain champion, competed in the Indoor Championships at Cobo Hall in Detroit, and shot in Las Vegas for money. I just don't do things in moderation and never have. And, later on, when I was coaching, it was the same, I was very into coaching and helping my teams win. In fact, I coached the first teams in the school history to win the city and conference championships. When I got into golf, couldn't just do it halfway. I excelled at the sport and got down to a three handicap. After I retired, I went into bass fishing and fished on the B.A.S.S. tour for eight or nine years and won one B.A.S.S. tournament. At that time, it was worth about $35,000. Nowadays, the winner gets $100,000.

So, I didn't do things in moderation and the same was true in the army. It's hard to explain. I didn't want to be there, but I was there and so I did the best I could. I was going to be there anyway, so I might as well fight the war as best as I could, be the best soldier I could be, the best leader. It was in my nature and being in the army and being in Vietnam wasn't going to change that. Besides doing my best could help me and the soldiers around me get home safely, which was our main goal.

When I was growing up, one of the things I read about and enjoyed were mountain men, the explorers of the Rocky Mountains who lived on their own in the wilderness in the 1800s. Being a soldier was the closest I could ever get to being a mountain man. Like them, I had to live by my wits, make trails with my machete, watch for signs of prey and predators – both being the VC.

For me, it was exciting. I enjoyed walking point. I'm not bragging, but I was good at it. For example, I actually learned how to smell the Vietcong. They had a distinctive scent, like charcoal. They cooked over charcoal and wood, so the smell of that smoke clung to them. Americans didn't smell like that, so I knew who it was when that scent hit my nostrils and I reacted accordingly. I'm sure they could smell us, too, whatever distinctive odor we had. Maybe we smelled like C rations. Having developed the skills to be a good point man was a matter of pride and satisfaction for me. Similar to being a champion archer, I wanted to be the best at walking point. I wanted the other soldiers to know they were in good hands when I was on point. I didn't want to be on point much more than my fair share – usually a third of the time – but when I had to be, it fed my self-esteem knowing that the other soldiers felt safer having me out front. In addition to the Silver Star, I also received an Air Medal, as mentioned before, and the Vietnam Campaign Medal. I'm not sure how much I earned them and how much I was just in the right place – or the wrong place. The Vietnam Campaign Medal really was just for being in the right place, because it was given to anyone who spent at least six months in country, regardless of what they did. It was kind of a participation trophy.

Did I get scared in battle? Yes, I got scared. Being good at my job didn't mean I wasn't scared. Actually, I was never scared at the time, during the battle. The fear would hit me the day after a battle, when it sunk in what could have happened. Postponing the fear was probably a defense mechanism or survival instinct. It didn't mean I was oblivious during a mission to the risks that were always there. Of course, I knew that even the best soldiers, the most skilled, could be victims of random bad luck, or of a well laid ambush, or a simply better fighter. The VC had the home field advantage and we all knew that. That gave them a clear edge over us. So, I was always scared at some level. Overcoming that fear was part of the excitement of war. That ability was another part of what made me good at my job. It wasn't something I could do completely or all the time, but enough to keep going, do well, and survive.

Basic training and AIT were kind of a brainwashing process that the army put us through, so we could do our jobs. It was a good thing. It enabled us to fight and kill people, to fire back when fired upon without hesitation, without thinking or deliberating. It kept us alive. It also made it possible for us to do something we had been conditioned all our lives not to do – kill other human beings. Without this conditioning, soldiers can't win and can't live through war. It's the way it's been throughout history.

I tell people that the greatest competition I was ever in, in my life, was a battle, a firefight. Battle held the highest stakes possible. If I lost, I didn't get to play the next day – or ever again. No sport had even been close to those stakes. In baseball, if we lost a game, we could shake it off and do better the next time. In bass fishing, if the fish weren't biting one day, they might the next. In war, if you didn't play at your highest level, you could very well be killed. There was no next game, if that happened. And, this went on every day for a year. Even on our standdown days, there was always a threat, a chance of enemy mortars, a possible surprise attack. This made war the most exciting activity ever. I've never done drugs, never smoked marijuana, or anything like that – in Vietnam, being high could get you killed – but I've never had a rush, excitement-wise, like I did in a battle. I don't believe that drugs could ever give a high that was close to the high of battle.

Along with always going overboard, I was not bashful. I don't know what it is about me, but I always did whatever I wanted to do. It almost never backfired on me. This was true throughout my life and carried over to Vietnam. I didn't mind asking to go see Artie at Phu Cat. I didn't mind asking for leave. I didn't mind asking for anything.

And, the other soldiers, who were less confident, would say, "God, how do you do that, Hoy?"

I'd answer, "I don't know, I just ask. All they can do is say no."

I did pretty much what I wanted to do and they left me alone. The fact that I willingly walked point – which most people avoided doing – and we all knew I was good at it probably helped when I asked for things. Like my old saying goes, "What are they going to do, send me to Nam and make me walk point?"

In reading these letters 50 years later, I was reminded that, when I first got over there, I didn't know what was going on and had to figure out how to fit in. I started learning as I went along and got better and better. I don't know when the point came that I felt like I had the hang of it, if that point ever did come, but I gradually felt a little more secure in what I was doing, like I had gotten my footing and wasn't floundering anymore. Later on, when I finally got situated and kind of knew what's going on, then my mind was on R&R. If I could just get to R&R and see Beth, all would be fine. After I got back from R&R, it was all about how many days were left until I could get out of there. The whole thing about the tour of duty in Vietnam was surviving the year. This was different from other wars. In World War II, they were there for the duration of the war. Same thing in Korea, the full duration. Those soldiers looked ahead to the end of the war. Let's win it and go home. Considering how long the Vietnam War turned out to be, it's a good thing that wasn't how the enlistments were handled. In Vietnam, you were there for one year, that was your tour of duty. Survive that and you were done. That was everybody's attitude, at least the ones that I knew, they just wanted to survive. How can I get over there, do my tour of duty, and get out to come back home? What else could people possibly be thinking about? Okay, maybe there were a few people who were interested in doing their part to stop the Communist domino expansion in southeast Asia. I never met them, though. I never heard a single conversation on that subject.

I was just recently married to a lovely wife – and we're still married after 54 years. Getting back to her was all I wanted to do, to get back to our life together and resume being a human being. That was the only thing that I really dwelled on over there. After R&R, my whole focus was on the fact that I was short (military term for having only a short time left in an assignment). I was getting short on time and I was doing things to get out of the field to increase my chances of surviving. So, I'd find ways to get back to the rear and not get shot at. I did everything I could to get through the tour of duty. And I did get through it. Even asking Artie to hide me up for seven days. People asked how in the world could I do that, how could I have the nerve to do it. I'd reply, well, I just did it. I just had no fear. Frankly, I had done more fighting and taken more risks than many of the people in that war, so I was completely okay with playing it a little safer near the end. My feeling was, what are they going to do to me? I didn't care how they might punish me, if it meant I was going to survive. I really wouldn't have minded if they had tossed me in the guard house and fed me three meals a day. That wouldn't have been too bad. But, they didn't do that. They didn't really even question me much about where I had been. The implied message I got from the leadership was, yes, I had done enough and deserved to get home to my wife. I agreed.

The thought of Vietnam, compared to other wars, is very upsetting. In Vietnam, we were pawns in a big chess game. As an infantryman, I was just a pawn, I was no more than that. If I got killed, they would just replace me with another pawn. That's the way battle was, they'd just stick us in there and if we got hit, they'd stick somebody else in. That's the way I felt, like they didn't really care about us. And, by "they," I mean the politicians in Washington, especially Johnson and McNamara, but also Congress and everyone else who decided we would fight and keep fighting this war.

Even worse, they didn't give us a chance to win. This has been a very common complaint among Vietnam veterans. Particularly after Tet, the political will to commit the resources needed to achieve victory was almost zero. If there had been a chance to win, if there was a purpose for what we were doing and we could win the war, our attitude would have been different. On the ground, it felt like we were winning ground. The battles I fought, overall, were wins. But, back home, the general public wasn't hearing about these. There was no chance of winning the war, even if we won the battles. The attitude of the Americans, back at that time, was we can solve everything at the conference table since Korea.

I got to Vietnam around the start of it. The war really got started back in 1964 and 1965. I got drafted in 1966 and arrived in 1967, when America was getting more involved and sending more and more troops over. Before that, we mostly had advisors over there training the South Vietnamese on how to fight. The advisors did a pretty good job of training them, but the South Vietnamese didn't do a very good job of fighting. Therefore, in 1965, General Westmoreland requested from President Johnson 100,000 additional troops. I was part of the 100,000 troops that they sent over. Of that 100,000, not all of them were in the field. As I talked about earlier, it's amazing how many people it takes in the rear to keep people in the field supplied and things going kind of smoothly. In 1967, he requested another 200,000 and eventually had troop level of over half a million. Not much later, though, his requests for more troops were denied and he was fired just a few months after I left Vietnam. You can imagine, he first said we'd need 100,000 more, then another 200,000, and then that was still not enough. What we really needed was to be allowed to invade North Vietnam and capture Hanoi and the rest of the country, and just wipe out the enemy force. That would've been fine. We could have won with that strategy. But, the politicians were scared of China, so that didn't happen. I'll explain why.

The DMZ was often referred to as the 17th parallel, where the latitudinal line of 17 degrees north passed through the narrow country. It was the military demarcation line between North and South

Vietnam established by the Geneva Accords of 1954. The line did not exactly coincide with the 17th parallel, but ran south of it, along the Ben Hai River to the village of Bo Ho Su and then west to the Laos border. It was called "demilitarized," because no military forces from either side were allowed within 3 miles north or south of the line. If you can't go into the zone, you can't cross it into the other side's territory. The North Vietnamese broke the spirit of that rule by establishing the Ho Chi Minh Trail through Laos and Cambodia to deliver troops, arms, and supplies to the Vietcong in South Vietnam. Meanwhile, we sat on the south side of the DMZ, like good boys.

People in American don't even realize why we had this DMZ. It was because of our experience in Korea, where we ended up with a DMZ along the 38th parallel, more or less. When the war broke out over there, North Korea pushed all the way down the peninsula through South Korea. We entered the war and pushed the North Koreans back all the way to the Yalu River, which separates Korea and China. China then joined in the fight and drove us back to the 38th parallel, which was almost exactly where things had been before the start of the war. What's north of Vietnam? China. So, a decade after Korea, we were afraid that, if we invaded North Vietnam, China would come into the war, like they had done in Korea. The Chinese had a military of 6 million. The number of Chinese troops in North Vietnam, even without us invading, was 170,000. We had about half a million troops in Vietnam at the height of the war, when I was there, and had our hands full with the Vietcong and North Vietnamese Army. We didn't want the Chinese increasing their forces in the country in response to us pushing north. So, we didn't. That kind of left us without a real mission. We weren't there to fight the war to win, to beat the North. I don't know why we're there. It just never made sense to me. We couldn't cross the DMZ, but the North could cross it and attack us and did so freely.

Our strategy seemed to be to just keep killing Vietcong. Our whole purpose was to search and destroy, to make contact with the enemy, no matter how big or how small and engage them in a fire-fight. The way the Vietcong look at the situation was, the Americans may have all the watches, but we have all the time. The American military didn't have time. Time was on the enemy's side, because America would not put up with a long war. Every American war within memory had been under four years – Korea, World War II, and World War I. We had had military advisors in Vietnam since 1959 and the war really escalated after the Gulf of Tonkin Incident in August 1964. So, by the time of the Tet Offensive, the war had been going on for 3½ years, really. America – American politicians and the American public – was done with Vietnam. In April 1967, General Westmoreland told Congress, "In evaluating the enemy strategy, it is evident to me that he believes our Achilles heel is our resolve. ... Your continued strong support is vital to the success of our mission." That strong support didn't continue much longer, if at all.

On top of the years was the number of casualties. When I arrived, there had been 8,407 Americans lost in the war (through 1966). In 1967, another 11,153 Americans were killed. 1968 was the worst year, with 16,592 American deaths. By the time Saigon fell in April 1975, another 21,000 Americans had died. I was there at just about the worst part of the war, as far as American deaths went. In the Korean War, we lost 36,516 men and women over just a couple years. (In Afghanistan and Iraq combined, about 6,700 American lives were lost over a span of 20 years, so far.)

On the other hand, the Vietnamese Communists had been fighting since 1945, first against the French and army of the former emperor of Vietnam. They were used to the fighting and could keep it up until we gave up. They predicted – correctly – that we wouldn't stick around for long. We didn't. We kept handing it over to the South Vietnamese and making them fight more and more and more. They couldn't handle it and ended up getting beat and we got out of there.

So, my attitude – as negative as it may have been when I was over there – was to survive. If we had had a chance of winning the war, my attitude would have been different, more positive. If we had a strategic objective – let's get this far north, then go here, and move to here, and here, so that we could make them surrender – then I would have understood better – at all – why we were there. But, we didn't have such an objective. It was a guerilla war without much in the way of observable tactical goals or gains.

Here's another thing that I feel is very important, maybe the most important thing, what I feel strongest about. This guerilla war was a time for the brass to play with new toys. The toys I'm talking about were the helicopters and airmobile tactics – us soldiers. We were the air calvary, the first air cavalry ever. We were the newest, shiniest toy. Back in horse and buggy time, when people were on horseback, the cavalry could move faster than foot soldiers, flank enemy, and go through the enemy. That's what the calvary was used for. The original cavalry was the charioteers way back in the 1500s BC. The use of cavalry for speed, mobility, range, and shock value continued through the Greeks, Romans, Middle Ages, and up through World War I. By World War II, horse cavalries were obsolete, replaced by vehicles, especially tanks for the shock value, which were referred to as armored cavalry. When we got to Nam, we had calvary again, but it was the helicopter. They could load us up on choppers and take us by air to drop in and engage the enemy – while simultaneously engaging them from the air – and do all kinds of different things tactically. This was even more speed, mobility, range, and shock value than any previous versions of cavalry. The military strategists must have been drooling over the thought of coming up with new ways to employ us. It was a tactician's theoretical dream come true. For us, though, there was nothing theoretical about it. We were the new toys for them and they enjoyed playing with us. It may have been war games for those academics, but it was not a game for us.

They had other new toys, including M16 rifles, M60 machine guns, M70 and M203 grenade launchers, Claymore mines, LAWs, M102 105 mm Howitzers, M109 155 mm Howitzers, M48 tanks, Cobra attack helicopters, and Puff the Magic Dragon, to name a few. Air assault was the favorite new toy out of all of these. This new 1st Air Cavalry Division, which was established in 1965 and sent to Vietnam, was like getting a giant chess set for Christmas, complete with two million pawns. It was one big experiment for the higher ups and we were the lab rats.

My feeling was that they had new weapons and saw this as a chance to go play with these doohickies at our expense. That's what has always bothered me more than anything else about the war, that you can take young Americans soldiers and put them in harm's way, while the people from West Point, Washington, and back in the rear made decisions that impacted the lives – or caused the deaths – of those young soldiers. The decisionmakers were so far removed from the people who were affected by their decisions that they didn't really have to view us as human beings. The troops were abstracts to them, not people they had to get to know. They didn't ever have to look us in the eyes and see our hopes and dreams – or our fear. They didn't have to hold the maimed bodies or the corpses in their arms and try to save them. They never had to watch the life leave a buddy's eyes. They didn't have to console the widows, parents, or children of the dead. They didn't have to help the injured to adapt to life in a wheelchair. They didn't have to lie next to us at night through recurring nightmares or face our anger during the day as PTSD caused irrational rage or depression caused suicidal thoughts. They didn't even have to explain to us why we weren't allowed to win the war. Instead, they had the luxury of sitting in their air-conditioned ivory towers and crystal cities and sacrifice the pawns on the chessboard on the other side of the globe. They weren't the ones out in the field getting shot at and getting shot. As I've said, the officers only had to stay in the field six months, while the enlisted men – the draftees – had to stay out there for a full year. What was the logic in that? What rationale could be used to justify this discrepancy? This was not a conversation that any officer chose to have with any of us. Instead, we were all flown to the brigade headquarters for the colonel's going away party, as if we gave a damn about him – or he gave a damn about any of us.

That's my complaint and my feeling about Vietnam and it's something that I don't want to forget and never will forget. People ask me how I can keep talking about this. I know a lot of people who can't talk about Vietnam and I understand that. Each person is different. I don't judge them for not talking about it and they probably don't judge me for being able and willing to talk about my experience. My view is, why would I want to forget something that helped make me who I am? It made me grow up, made me more mature. It gave me more of a sense of responsibility and more faith in my abilities. It made me believe in myself more and want to take charge of my life and do something with it. It made me value more the time I have on earth, the time I get to spend with Beth. When I came back home, I had some goals for my life other than just to play baseball. It that sense, the Vietnam War was the best thing that happened to me. That's how I felt then and how I still feel. I probably would feel differently if I had come back without an arm or leg or wounded or something, I'm sure my attitude might have been different. As it stands, what I've described are my feelings on Vietnam in the military.

I can't talk about Afghanistan or Iraq. The U.S. military that fought those wars wasn't made up of draftees. The army we have nowadays is made up of people who joined. It was their choice to sign up. We weren't given that choice, most of us. So, the recent veterans' attitude may be different than mine was in Nam in many ways. Their attitude might be the same as mine about many things, but that's for them to say. My story, my experience, and my feelings are as expressed in this book. Nam was a completely different deal than the recent wars. I have great respect for today's soldiers, even though our experiences and maybe our feelings aren't exactly the same.

# CHAPTER 18

AFTER I GOT out of the service, I returned to college on the G.I. Bill and earned my degree in physical education, then got a teaching job in Clovis. I am grateful for the encouragement and assistance of Professor Fergus, who helped me quite a bit in my studies. He was a very sharp guy and we became very good friends.

While in that teaching job during the day, I got a master's degree through night school and summer school, which raised my salary. I was a PE teacher and coached boys football and basketball at Yucca Junior High in Clovis. Many years later, I coached girls basketball at Hot Springs High School in Truth or Consequences, New Mexico. Beth was also a PE teacher, at Marshall Junior High in Clovis, and played competitive volleyball on a championship team. Beth and I both taught archery – we had both been state champions – for the Clovis summer youth program. After 23 years of teaching, added to the two years of military service, I had 25 years in and could retire at age 50.

That's when I got into bass fishing. I even invented a fishing lure, which I named the Devils Claw. I also took a lot of art classes and I paint now and have done quite a lot of paintings. In fact, at age 78, ten of my paintings were selected for an exhibit at the Memorial Medical Center in Las Cruces, New Mexico, along with art by 20 artists from all over the state. As I said before, I don't do anything in moderation. I get involved in something and I go after it wholeheartedly.

Our life has been great and people ask, "How did you survive that year being apart after only being married for a couple of months before he had to leave?" I don't know how to answer that. In fact, I don't know whether we survived it or not. I don't know that we would describe it that way. That's just the way things were with us, back then and now. We were brought up, and it has always been this way, with our whole philosophy being that, if you love somebody, you get married and love them for the rest of your life. Why get married if you don't love the person? And, if you love them, you keep loving them. We loved each other then and we love each other now. It's never changed. Yeah, it was trying on us, but we were young and had no fears of anything. We just did what we wanted to do. And, we worked out. I can't tell you anything else. It's just what we do, how we live. Yeah, we've had some arguments. I think we've had about three or four arguments in 54 years of marriage and I think they were all over my Dad. (Beth laughs in agreement.) Like with anyone else, we've had some things that have happened that we've had to get through. We just get through them together, no matter what. There's no other option for us.

She brought up one point that I never even thought of. I don't think there's been a time that we've gone to bed at night without kissing each other good night and telling each other, "I love you." Even if we went to bed mad – which happened very few times – we would still kiss each other and say, "I love you." That's been every night for over half a century and we still do that to this day. It was a love that was meant to be, I guess. I don't know how else to say it but that we love each other.

We've talked about how, when you get married, you love each other, but you really don't know how much you love each other until years and years and years and years pass. Each year I think our love grew and grew and grew and grew. In some marriages, it dissipates, but ours never did at all, not even a little bit. The opposite happened with us. In addition to loving each other, we like each other. We like being with each other. We've always done everything together – because we always wanted to be together. When we were apart, at work or for any reason, we looked forward to being together again. We could hardly imagine being separated for any period of time. My hobbies became her hobbies and her hobbies became my hobbies. Whatever interested her would interest me, and vice versa.

We went hunting together. I was going to go hunting and she said, "Do you mind if I go hunting with you?"

I said, "No, honey, I don't mind at all. Get your butt in the car. Let's go." Her big complaint was, if we would go hunting and there was a mountain, that I had to climb the mountain to the other side. If we came from the other side of the mountain, I'd have to climb over the first side. Either way. This was another example of me not doing anything in moderation.

I'd go bass fishing and she'd go with me and ask, "Well, if we put the boat in at this end of the lake will you have to go to the other end of the lake?"

I said, "Yes, ma'am, that's the way it is. If I put in at the other end, I'll have to come all the way to this end." It just seemed I always had to run the farthest part there was. Still, she just accepts it and goes along with me with an amused smile.

And, dove hunting. We hunted dove together. We also quail hunted. We sandhill crane hunted. We duck hunted. We goose hunted. We prairie chicken hunted. We pheasant hunted. If it flew, we hunted it. Beth was on every hunting trip with us. Everything we've ever done has pretty much been together and it still is to this day. If I went fishing with somebody else in a small boat for two, we'd get in the boat and Beth would put us both in the water, then she'd come back at the end of the day and pick us up.

When we fished professionally, we traveled together and we took turns driving. We'd drive 12, 14 hours a day going to the destination. We got to see the country together when we were bass fishing, all up and down the east coast. We found places we wouldn't want to live, over there on the East coast. We love it here in New Mexico and those trips confirmed that we were in the right place for us.

That's been our life and it still is and it will be that way forever on. Our love has been such that we do things together and we've always done things together.

We're making this book together. Ty and Karen Pierce – he's kind of our adopted son, in our own way, through coaching – talked us into putting this story together and that's what we've done. The four of us went through all the old letters and got them organized by date. For the storytelling, maybe I've done the most of it, but Beth and I talk about it back and forth and she reads what I write and gives me feedback, corrections, and suggestions. She's always right, too. I value her input more than anyone else's, because she knows me and our story better than anyone else.

One other thing, no one teaches courtesy and politeness anymore, but Beth and I still always practice it, especially to each other. To this day, I say "yes, ma'am" to her and she says "yes, sir" to me. It's not out of anything but politeness, respect, and love for each other. The same with "please" and "thank you." I also open the door for her and just do stuff that I'm supposed to be doing as a matter of common courtesy for the woman I love. It doesn't matter to us if these manners have disappeared from the rest of society, it's still part of how we show our love for each other.

Like Beth's Mom always said: "yes ma'am, no ma'am, thank you, please. Always use those words."

Thank you. I love you, Beth.